Cambridge Elements

Elements in New Religious Movements

Series Editor
Rebecca Moore
San Diego State University

Founding Editor
†James R. Lewis
Wuhan University

J. KRISHNAMURTI

Self-Inquiry, Awakening, and Transformation

Constance A. Jones
California Institute of Integral Studies

CAMBRIDGE
UNIVERSITY PRESS

Shaftesbury Road, Cambridge CB2 8EA, United Kingdom

One Liberty Plaza, 20th Floor, New York, NY 10006, USA

477 Williamstown Road, Port Melbourne, VIC 3207, Australia

314–321, 3rd Floor, Plot 3, Splendor Forum, Jasola District Centre, New Delhi – 110025, India

103 Penang Road, #05–06/07, Visioncrest Commercial, Singapore 238467

Cambridge University Press is part of Cambridge University Press & Assessment, a department of the University of Cambridge.

We share the University's mission to contribute to society through the pursuit of education, learning and research at the highest international levels of excellence.

www.cambridge.org
Information on this title: www.cambridge.org/9781009494717

DOI: 10.1017/9781009337762

© Constance A. Jones 2025

This publication is in copyright. Subject to statutory exception and to the provisions of relevant collective licensing agreements, no reproduction of any part may take place without the written permission of Cambridge University Press & Assessment.

When citing this work, please include a reference to the DOI 10.1017/9781009337762

First published 2025

A catalogue record for this publication is available from the British Library

ISBN 978-1-009-49471-7 Hardback
ISBN 978-1-009-33775-5 Paperback
ISSN 2635-232X (online)
ISSN 2635-2311 (print)

Cambridge University Press & Assessment has no responsibility for the persistence or accuracy of URLs for external or third-party internet websites referred to in this publication and does not guarantee that any content on such websites is, or will remain, accurate or appropriate.

J. Krishnamurti

Self-Inquiry, Awakening, and Transformation

Elements in New Religious Movements

DOI: 10.1017/9781009337762
First published online: January 2025

Constance A. Jones
California Institute of Integral Studies
Author for correspondence: Constance A. Jones, conniej3g@gmail.com

Abstract: This Element explores the life, teaching, and legacy of philosopher and spiritual teacher Jiddu Krishnamurti. From an obscure childhood in south India, he was "discovered" at age fourteen by the Theosophical Society as the vehicle for the prophesied World Teacher of this cosmic age. At age thirty-four, he disaffiliated from the Society, became an independent teacher, and, for sixty years, traveled widely and addressed thousands of audiences on the need to develop awareness and attention for transformation of consciousness. His teaching defines the human condition as perilous, dominated almost completely by cultural and personal conditioning, fear, and negative emotions. Freedom from these perils, his teaching states, occurs through rigorous self-observation and inquiry in the search for truth. While extremely popular, Krishnamurti rejected the mantle of authority invariably attributed to spiritual masters and teachers. He created schools in his name to implement his pedagogy of non-authoritarianism and freedom from conditioning.

Keywords: Krishnamurti, self-inquiry, personal freedom, consciousness, conditioning, World Teacher

© Constance A. Jones 2025

ISBNs: 9781009494717 (HB), 9781009337755 (PB), 9781009337762 (OC)
ISSNs: 2635-232X (online), 2635-2311 (print)

Contents

	Introduction	1
1	Boyhood and Early Life with the Theosophical Society	3
2	An Independent Teacher (1929–1986)	18
3	The Context: Teacher and Teaching	21
4	The Religious Life	30
5	Meditation in Everyday Life	38
6	Transformation	45
7	Scholarly Encounters	49
8	Education as Religion	61
9	Krishnamurti's Legacy	67
	References	71

Introduction

This Element introduces the life and teachings of philosopher and teacher Jiddu Krishnamurti (1895–1986), a South Asian from India who offered a unique perspective on expansion of human consciousness. His message centers on individual self-inquiry as the only practice useful for discovering freedom from the conditioning of society and for ultimate self-realization.

Described as "the quintessential iconoclast of the twentieth century" (Sanat 1999: xi) and "the eminent thinker of our age" (Mehta 1987: 54), Krishnamurti, by any measure, led an extraordinary life. After a somewhat obscure childhood in south India, he attained international notoriety at age fourteen when he was identified by the Theosophical Society as the vehicle for the prophesied World Teacher of this cosmic age. Before reaching adulthood, he was venerated and served as head of a worldwide order established in his name. After twenty years Krishnamurti disbanded the order and became a teacher in his own right, without benefit of any organization. For more than sixty years on a public circuit, he addressed thousands of audiences, primarily in India, England, the United States, and Europe, and met with scholars and practitioners in several fields for dialogues, aimed at observing consciousness in the moment through collaborative inquiry. His teaching and his personality influenced world leaders in politics, science, religion, and philosophy, and his writings continue to be cited for their insights into the human condition (see Figure 1).

Section 1 traces Krishnamurti's childhood, his appointment by the Theosophical Society as the vehicle for the prophesied World Teacher, and the onset in 1922 of the transformative Process that affected his entire being. Section 2 explains his life as a teacher after 1929 when he disbanded the order instituted in his name and became an independent teacher. Section 3 contextualizes his teaching within his life, aligning elements of his message with his personal experience. Section 4 explores Krishnamurti's definition of the religious life as a principle of unification that transforms the habitual fragmentation of the psyche into a mind characterized by wholeness and order. Section 5 describes Krishnamurti's commitment to the possibility of an unconditioned mind, a state of persistent meditation in everyday life, that can open all individuals to the search for truth through engagement with the unknown. Section 6 explores his teaching about human possibilities of transformation, which include the identification of each person with the whole, summarized by his phrase "you are the world." Section 7 examines Krishnamurti's engagement with scientists and philosophers, particularly highlighting his dialogues with theoretical physicist David Bohm. Section 8 analyzes his educational philosophy and looks at the ways in which education can lead to personal liberation and transformation. Section 9 summarizes the legacy of Krishnamurti's teachings.

Figure 1 J. Krishnamurti, 1982. Courtesy Woodfin Camp and Associates, New York.

This Element argues that the life and teachings of Krishnamurti are so intertwined, that he does not represent any tradition of self-realization or identifiable cosmology, but rather teaches directly out of his own insights. What he discovered himself aligns clearly with nondual philosophies of enlightenment that call upon each individual to search for truth and be responsible for their own trajectory through life. Because he did not establish a formal organization or proselytize for a defined membership, however, the scope of his influence is not easily delineated, lying primarily within informal exposure to his message. Research into his life reveals controversies, described herein, which pertain to the details of his personal experiences, the content of his teaching, his unique presentation, and his prescribed methods. These controversies are presented without providing a final determination.

Sources

This Element relies on several types of resources for its content – biographies, Krishnamurti's personal journals, reminiscences by associates, audio and video tapes of addresses and dialogues, and commentaries on the teaching. Reports of his life draw primarily from two sources. First, the comprehensive biographies by Mary Lutyens (1908–1999) (1975, 1983, 1988, 1990, 1996), daughter of Lady Emily Lutyens (1874–1964), one of Krishnamurti's closest friends, and Edwin

Lutyens (1869–1944), architect and designer of New Delhi, the capital of independent India. Mary Lutyens grew up alongside Krishnamurti from 1911 when she was three years old (Lutyens 1975: ix). Second, the biography and dialogues reported by Pupul Jayakar (1915–1997) (1986, 1995), who met Krishnamurti in India in the 1940s and served as his intellectual amanuensis, watching over him through a recurrence of the mysterious "Process" in 1948 (Jayakar 1986, 1995). Both Lutyens and Jayakar note the development of Krishnamurti's teaching as largely a function of the challenges and lessons met in his own life's trajectory. Other less comprehensive biographies and reminiscences by associates also contribute to the depiction of Krishnamurti's life.

Accounts of the teaching itself draw from a variety of sources: Krishnamurti's own writings and personal journals; recordings and transcriptions of his talks and dialogues; scholarly analyses (both appreciative and critical) by academics, scientists, and educators; descriptions of the schools and foundations organized in his name; and reflections by those who have observed his teaching in their lives. Primary and secondary literature concerning his influence on the study of consciousness and transformation, his demonstration of dialogical exchange in his teaching, and the dialogical process developed with David Bohm are also utilized.

The published corpus is vast, including 107 books currently in print (some of which are translated into 31 languages), 600 videos, and 2,500 audio recordings, mainly derived from lectures Krishnamurti gave over his lengthy career (Lee 2024). The talks, all delivered in English, invariably cover wide-ranging topics so that any single talk might span the breadth of his teaching – from the function of thought to an analysis of global disharmony (Van der Struijf & Van der Struijf 2000). Almost all public addresses given by Krishnamurti in his later life are available in audio and video formats. Additionally, two full-length films review his life and teaching (Mendizza 1985, 1990).

Along with other foundations relating to Krishnamurti and his teachings that exist around the world, the Krishnamurti Foundation of America (KFA, www.kfa.org) maintains a library, bookstore, archive, and web presence. The KFA's presence on the internet includes current usage of Facebook (300 K followers), Instagram (206 K followers), TikTok (48.9 K followers), YouTube (1.5 M views), the KFA Newsletter (66.5 K subscribers), and "The Immeasurable" (7.9 K users) (Lee 2024).

1 Boyhood and Early Life with the Theosophical Society

Jiddu Krishnamurti was born in 1895 in Madanapalle, Madras Presidency (now Andhra Pradesh), into a Telugu-speaking Brahmin family steeped in the traditions of Hinduism and a sacred view of the world. His great-grandfather had been an eminent Sanskrit scholar and his grandfather also a learned man and civil servant in colonial India. His father, Jiddu Narianiah (d. 1924), a graduate of Madras University, served in the Indian Civil Service as an official in the Revenue Department and later as District Magistrate (Lutyens 1975: 1). Krishnamurti's mother, Sanjeevamma (d. 1905), was a pious and charitable woman known for her devout nature, psychic gifts, and paranormal visions. She had a premonition that her eighth child would be in some way remarkable and insisted that the baby be born in the *puja* room, a special room set aside in orthodox Hindu households for prayers, usually proscribed for any polluting activity such as childbirth (Jayakar 1986: 15–16). Consistent with orthodox Hindu tradition, immediately after birth, Krishnamurti's horoscope was cast by an astrologer, who predicted that the child would become a great teacher, but only after encountering significant obstacles (Jayakar 1986: 16). According to Hindu observance, six days after the birth of a child, the important name-giving ceremony is held. Jiddu Narianiah and Sanjeevamma, following tradition, named their eighth child "Krishnamurti" (literally "the image of Krishna") after the Lord Krishna, himself an eighth child (Jayakar 1986: 17).

At the age of six, Krishnamurti went through the sacred thread ceremony, *upanayana* – initiation into the first of four stages of life of a twice-born male or *brahmacharya*, specified in ancient custom for all Brahmin boys at the beginning of their life of study and discipline (Jayakar 1986: 17). As part of the initiation ceremony, the Hindu priest placed the sacred thread over Krishnamurti's right shoulder and his father whispered the sacred Gayatri Mantra – invocation to the sun – into his ear. According to Narianiah, "It is a ceremony which Brahmin boys go through when it is time to launch them out into the world of education" (Jayakar 1986: 17). After the initiation ceremony, the young boy was taken to a Hindu temple for prayers and then on to the nearest school and "handed over to the teacher" (Lutyens 1975: 3) to begin his education. All these rituals are integral to the orthodox Brahmin tradition of Hinduism and Krishnamurti's family strictly observed each rite.

As Brahmins, the Jiddu family belonged to a high caste, the significance of which cannot be overstated. Brahmins represent a spiritual rather than an economic elite and constitute, according to Hindu tradition, the hereditary group that has arrived, through karma and reincarnation, at the last and highest stratum of spiritual evolution. Traditionally, they are considered purer in mind and body than the lower castes and thus constitute the caste from which temple priests and religious scholars derive (Lutyens 1975: 2). Throughout his childhood, Krishnamurti's life was circumscribed by the conventions of caste and "the rituals, theology, and ethics of Hinduism would have been second nature to him, a matter of domestic routine" (Vernon 2000: 27–8).

The young Krishnamurti was physically delicate and suffered several recurring illnesses, including malaria. Repetitive bouts of fever combined with Narianiah's frequent transfers of residence interrupted the boy's schooling so that "in lessons he fell far behind other boys his age" (Lutyens 1975: 4). A quiet and contemplative child, often lost in dreamy imaginings, he drew negative judgments, including inferior mental functioning, from his teachers and peers. His mother seems to be the one person who appreciated his unusual behavior and saw his dreaminess as a type of gift, rather than stubbornness or lack of intelligence (Vernon 2000: 28). Krishnamurti relates that his happiest memories of childhood center around the time spent with his mother, who would conduct Hindu worship, *puja*, in the family shrine, send him out to distribute rice to beggars, and teach him about karma and reincarnation. After his mother's death, he saw his mother's image in visions, a fact confirmed by his father Narianiah (Lutyens 1975: 4–6).

Up to the age of ten, when Krishnamurti's mother died, the family was intact. Throughout his first ten years, both his father and mother taught him at home, adhered to Brahminical practices, and introduced him to the teaching of the Theosophical Society. His father attended conventions of the Society in Madras and held meetings at the family home for the study of Theosophical ideas (Krishnamurti in Jayakar 1986: 19).

Both parents respected Annie Besant (1847–1933), who became president of the Theosophical Society in 1907 and, as described later, was to become the adoptive mother for Krishnamurti and his brother Nityananda, and a central figure in Krishnamurti's life until her death in 1933. In 1907 after the death of his wife, Narianiah wrote to Besant "to offer his 'whole-hearted and full time service' in any capacity in exchange for free accommodation for himself and his sons in the Compound of the international Headquarters of the Society at Adyar near Madras" (Lutyens 1975: 7). After an initial rejection of this request, Besant agreed to accept his services and in January, 1909, Narianiah took a position as assistant secretary in the Theosophical Society and moved with his four sons to the international headquarters of the Theosophical Society at Adyar, outside Madras (now Chennai), India (Lutyens 1975: 7).

The Theosophical Society

The Theosophical Society, founded in 1875 in New York City by Helena Petrovna Blavatsky (1831–1891), Henry Steel Olcott (1832–1907), and William Q. Judge (1851–1896), began as an organization dedicated to a synthesis of science, religion, and philosophy with the credo, "There is no religion higher than truth." The founders sought to promote the study of insights from various world religions, investigate occult phenomena, and foster the brotherhood of all humankind.

The Theosophical Society with international headquarters at Adyar, in Tamil Nadu state, defines its teaching not as a religion per se, but rather as a restatement of the essence of religion itself by affirming three objectives:

1. to form a nucleus of the Universal Brotherhood of Humanity without distinction of race, creed, sex, caste, or color;
2. to encourage the study of Comparative Religion, Philosophy, and Science; and
3. to investigate unexplained laws of nature and the powers latent in humans. (Lutyens 1975: 10)

The Preamble to the bylaws refers to the hope of penetrating further than science into "the esoteric philosophies of ancient times" (Campbell 1980: 28).

Although Olcott became the first president (1875–1907), the writings and teachings of Blavatsky became synonymous with the tenets of the Society. The Society accepted Blavatsky's self-description as a disciple of highly evolved beings, *mahatmas* or Masters of Wisdom, who had instructed her in esoteric truths that she referred to as the ancient wisdom, the secret doctrine, or Theosophy (meaning divine wisdom). Her reports include personal contacts with an occult brotherhood of these Masters made during her travels in the Far East, particularly in the Himalayas (Campbell 1980: 54–61). Their teachings, Blavatsky states, deemed to be perennial truths and the universal basis of all valid religions, were transmitted directly to her and became the basis of her writings (Murphet 1975; Campbell 1980), most notably *Isis Unveiled* (Blavatsky 1877) and *The Secret Doctrine: The Synthesis of Science, Religion and Philosophy* (Blavatsky 1888), which remain foundational to the Society's ontology and cosmology.

Even within Theosophical circles, Blavatsky's narratives of her travel to the Himalayas and her direct tutelage by the Masters there have been surrounded by doubt and controversy, based primarily on independent scholarly investigation of the content of the writings themselves as well as lack of any independent sources to validate her claims (Campbell 1980: 56–61). Challenges to her personal narrative as well as the content of the teaching include charges of plagiarism, unacknowledged Western esoteric roots – particularly Masonry and Rosicrucianism – and inconsistencies in the universal wisdom proffered by the Masters, alleged to be omniscient (Campbell 1980: 56–61; Godwin 1994: 326–8; Washington 1995: 26–46). Even though questions persist concerning Blavatsky's biographical narrative, the provenance of received truths, and her idiosyncratic approach to occult communication, the existence of the Masters and continuing communication from them remain central to the perspectives of most Theosophists (Campbell 1980: 60–1, 178–87). From the earliest days of Blavatsky's personal narrative, two Masters figure prominently in Theosophical thought – Kuthumi (Koot Hoomi) and Morya – both of whom also appear in the life of the young Krishnamurti as he was schooled at Adyar (Lutyens 1975: 10–11; Campbell 1980: 81).

After 1879 when Blavatsky and Olcott traveled together to India and began to champion Indian aspirations for political unification and a revival of the Indian people's pride in the history, religion, and culture of their country, the Society attracted educated and influential British colonialists as well as Indians as members (Campbell 1980: 78–83). Further, in 1880, they were welcomed in Ceylon (now Sri Lanka) as Western champions of Buddhism as they worked with Sinhalese Buddhists in efforts to limit the influence of Christian evangelism, considered prejudicial and vituperative (Campbell 1980: 83–7). As Olcott stated, the Society in its commitment to no particular religion was "as loyally working with Indians to promote Hinduism as it had been with the Sinhalese Buddhists to revive Buddhism" (Olcott cited in Campbell 1980: 86).

Interest in Theosophical principles grew in America, Europe, and India. In large part, Theosophical ideas are consistent with the cosmological and psychological teachings of Hinduism and Buddhism – with explorations into esoteric Christianity – and are portrayed in an amalgam of Hindu and Buddhist terminology, particularly using the concepts of evolution, karma, and reincarnation (Hanegraaff 2006: 1114–21; Jones & Ryan 2007: 444–5). The synthesis of East and West, religion and science, as well as spiritual and educational understanding, made Theosophy attractive to cosmopolitan, liberal people of many nationalities who had been disappointed by the dogmatism of both religion and science. These progressives sought to unite the diverse peoples of the world in a peaceful brotherhood (Hanegraaff 2006: 1114–16).

Part of Theosophical teaching, from the time of Blavatsky and creation of the Society's Preamble, is the exploration of occult and clairvoyant powers for discovering the hidden mysteries of nature and the esoteric powers of humanity. Founding Theosophists used their understanding of esotericism to draw from a host of related movements that included the occult sciences of astrology, alchemy, ritual magic, divination, Spiritualism, and psychism as well as distinct movements such as Gnosticism, Pythagoreanism, Neo-Platonism, Hermeticism, Kabbalah, and Rosicrucianism (Godwin 1994: 277–362). Foundational to the diversity in these movements is the esoteric assertion that an individual can comprehend symbol, myth, and ultimate reality only through a personal struggle for progressive illumination on successive levels (Faivre and Needleman 1995: xii). This personal struggle involves "functioning effectively in the external world and ... submitting oneself to a more conscious and transcendent reality that is contacted within the self" (Faivre and Needleman 1995: xxvi).

Theosophy combined these tenets of Western esotericism with Buddhist and Hindu ontologies to form a worldview that includes a complex cosmology, a metaphysical psychology, an esoteric physiology, and an evolutionary scheme that encompasses eons of cosmic and planetary changes. Esoteric tenets from the West meshed well with Theosophical understanding of Asian concepts of reincarnation, karma, and progression through spiritual evolution toward self-realization (de Purucker 1979). For understanding and practice of the tenets of esotericism, Olcott in 1888 ordered formation of an Esoteric Section of the Theosophical Society, which "legitimated Madame Blavatsky's desire to pursue occult instruction with an elite group within the Society" (Campbell 1980: 98). Blavatsky herself acted as leader, "known as the Outer Head – the Inner Heads being the Mahatmas (Masters) with whom she was supposed to have direct ties" (Hanegraaff 2006: 1119). Although multiple divisions and dissensions have surrounded the operation of both the Esoteric Section and the Theosophical Society since their beginnings (Godwin 1994: 362; Hanegraaff 2006: 1119), the section has endured until today, operating in secret with its own order of practices and rituals.

The combination of an esoteric worldview, belief in an occult hierarchy, and the Indian, European, and American community of seekers brought together in the Society constituted the milieu in which the young Krishnamurti was immersed in the next two decades of his life, from 1909 to 1929 (Lutyens 1975; Campbell 1980: 120–50; Jones 2010).

Discovery of the Vehicle for the World Teacher

In 1889, Annie Besant, a prominent figure in progressive movements in England, who would become central to the workings of the Society as a whole and Krishnamurti's life in particular, read Blavatsky's *Secret Doctrine*, an act that would change her life in significant ways. Besant (née Wood) was born in 1847 in London, raised in the Church of England, married a minister in the church, and bore two children. With each passing year, her unhappiness in marriage, the severe illnesses of her children, her acute observations of the social inequities surrounding her, and her own diligent inquiries into theological questions prompted her to question the doctrines of the church on many grounds (Wessinger 1988: 41–64). She left her husband and became a "passionate crusader for freedom of thought, women's rights, trade unionism, Fabian socialism, and birth control" (Jayakar 1986: 22). Self-identified as an atheist, she used her considerable gift as an orator to deliver public addresses on reform of many social ills. But, upon reading Blavatsky's work, she "turned her enormous energies from materialism and atheism to the pursuit of the occult and sacred" (Jayakar 1986:

22). She soon joined the Theosophical Society, became the most favored protégé of Blavatsky, and joined the Inner Group of the Esoteric Section of the Theosophical Society, which functioned to maintain contact with the Masters (Wessinger 1988: 65–6).

Besant took up residence at the headquarters of the International Society at Adyar and became its president in 1907. She continued her work for social reform begun in the United Kingdom by working to improve social conditions in India, founding many schools, and leading in the movement for Indian Home Rule (Wessinger 1988: 2–3). Although not a supporter of Mahatma Gandhi's *satyagraha* (nonviolent resistance) campaign, her participation in Indian politics as a moderate proponent of Home Rule led to her popularity, and she was elected the first woman president of the National Congress of 1918 (Wessinger 1988: 2–3).

Alongside these extraordinary achievements, Besant at the same time was convinced of India's special role in spiritual evolution. She spoke of her conviction that India's mission in the world is to share its genius for religious and spiritual knowledge (Jayakar 1986: 22–3).

> If religion perish here, it will perish everywhere and in India's hand is laid the sacred charge of keeping alight the torch of spirit amid the fogs and storms of increasing materialism. If that torch drops from her hands, its flame will be trampled out by the feet of hurrying multitudes, eager for worldly goods; and India, bereft of spirituality, will have no future, but will pass on into the darkness, as Greece and Rome have passed. (Besant 1889: n.p.)

Underlying Besant's fervor for India's mission was another prediction for world change. Termed "progressive messianism" (Wessinger 1988: 27), Besant's perspective entailed "a progressive and evolutionary view of history with the hope for a terrestrial salvation that will be accomplished imminently by a messiah who will enter the historical process to effect a radical but non-catastrophic change" (Wessinger 1988: 27).

Besant accepted Blavatsky's complex evolutionary scheme involving sequential "Root Races" (or dispensations) of humanity with members of the Occult Hierarchy officiating to usher in each new dispensation. According to Besant, Blavatsky's secret teachings, given only to her advanced students, specified that the "inner purpose of the Society was to prepare the world for the coming of a new Race" and identified Master Kuthumi and Master Morya as the two Teachers who would officiate at the coming of the new age (Wessinger 1988: 275–6).

But it was Besant who would use her own occult powers (Wessinger 1988: 279) and research skills to enhance Blavatsky's description of the advent of a new civilization, by predicting the appearance of a World Teacher, or

Bodhisattva, to usher in the new Root Race. According to Besant, a "World Teacher appeared on earth every time a sub-race was beginning" and, further, "all religions were delivered by a World Teacher" (Wessinger 1988: 270–5). Besant placed this emissary above the Masters in the Occult Hierarchy in a more distinctive rank – that of World Teacher or Lord Maitreya, the same consciousness that inhabited Lord Krishna in Hinduism and Jesus Christ in Christianity. This consciousness, she predicted, would soon incarnate into a contemporary person, who would serve as the "vehicle" of the World Teacher to bring a new teaching on a global scale (Lutyens 1975: 11). According to her insights, the World Teacher for the Sixth Root Race would be characterized by love and service, similar to the principle of a Bodhisattva, rather than the characterization of the Teacher of the previous Fifth Root Race, who was characterized by mind (Wessinger 1988: 270–7).

Besant saw her most important personal contribution to this messianic narrative to be preparation of the world for the appearance of the World Teacher (Wessinger, 1988: 270–1). In 1896, five years after Blavatsky's death, Besant publicly affirmed this expectation of a World Teacher, who would arrive imminently (Lutyens 1975: 12–13).

Besant was soon joined in leading the Theosophical anticipation of welcoming the World Teacher by another British citizen, a former Anglican clergyman with reputed powers of clairvoyance, Charles Webster Leadbeater (1854–1934). Ordained to the priesthood of the Church of England in 1879, Leadbeater drew upon his already avid interest in the supernatural and Spiritualism when he read the stories of Blavatsky's contact with the Masters (Tillett 1982: 26) and made her acquaintance in 1884 in London. The very next year in Blavatsky's presence, Leadbeater experienced his first meeting with a Master named Dwal Khul, which began a communication with other Masters that was to continue until his death (Tillett 1982: 39). According to Leadbeater's primary biographer, Blavatsky "totally transformed and remade his personality, changing him from an ordinary curate ... into a pupil of the Masters" (Tillett 1982: 40).

Although Besant and Leadbeater had met in 1894 in England, it was in 1909 that Leadbeater settled into the routine of Theosophical life at Adyar when he took charge of *The Theosophist*, a journal published by the Society, and began to document his occult investigations (Tillett 1982: 102). In regular talks and writings, he came increasingly to identify himself as an occultist who claimed "regular communication [through clairvoyance] with the Powers that govern the earth from the Inner Planes, the Masters or Mahatmas, the Supermen who constitute the Occult Hierarchy of the planet" (Tillett 1982: 1) – the same mahatmas who Blavatsky reports taught her the mysteries of the universe (Campbell 1980: 53–6).

Figure 2 J. Krishnamurti, c. 1924. Photo by Albert Witzel, courtesy the Krishnamurti Foundation of America.

In April 1909 during a swim with his young assistants at the Theosophical estate at Adyar, Leadbeater had a chance encounter with Krishnamurti and his younger brother Nityananda (1898–1925). While Leadbeater's companions were drawn to the outgoing Nityananda, Leadbeater focused on the more withdrawn older brother (see Figure 2) and reported that the boy "had the most wonderful aura he had ever seen, without a particle of selfishness in it ... and that one day the boy would become a spiritual teacher and great orator" (Lutyens 1975: 21). Leadbeater's fascination could not have been based on Krishnamurti's outward appearance, as he was "under-nourished, scrawny and dirty" and his "vacant expression gave him an almost moronic look" (Lutyens 1975: 21). Yet, Leadbeater soon declared "that the boy was to be the vehicle for the Lord Maitreya 'unless something went wrong' and that he, Leadbeater, had been directed to help train him for that purpose" (Lutyens 1975: 21).

Besant was informed of and accepted Leadbeater's "discovery" of Krishnamurti as indeed the vehicle of the awaited World Teacher, which, in effect, ousted Hubert van Hook, previously selected by Besant as the possible vehicle (Lutyens 1983: 24–5). Krishnamurti and Nityananda were then removed from their school, given residence at the Theosophical headquarters in Adyar, and instructed personally by Leadbeater. According to Leadbeater, he would take the boy Krishnamurti every night in his astral body during sleep to learn from Master Kuthumi. Each subsequent morning, Krishnamurti would write notes about the meeting with Master Kuthumi, but because the boy's English was not excellent, Leadbeater edited the notes to make sure that no mistakes were included. Leadbeater then typed the notes himself and finally took the manuscript clairvoyantly to Master Kuthumi and even to the Lord Maitreya himself for validation (Leadbeater in Tillett 1982: 135–9). Concerning his tutelage, Krishnamurti later related that he "began to see the Master K. H. [Kuthumi] in the form put before me. Later on, as I grew, I began to see the Lord Maitreya ... (and later) the Buddha" (Lutyens 1983: 13).

Beginning in the 1890s, Leadbeater had conducted research into the past lives of Society members – a project that became his preoccupation once Krishnamurti was identified as the vehicle. Using clairvoyance, Leadbeater identified the particulars of thirty lives of Alcyone (Tillett 1982: 108), the name given to Krishnamurti throughout his successive lives – enough to fill two large volumes (Besant and Leadbeater 1924). The method by which Leadbeater received these details was observed as identical to any author dictating his creative works to a secretary, that is, completely unverified by any other observer (Nethercot 1963: 141). For this reason, the transmissions received by Leadbeater as well as his regular communications with the Masters were held in suspicion by many in the Society and prompted charges of deliberate fakery (Tillett 1982: 114–15). Others, including Besant, defended Leadbeater's integrity and the extent of his clairvoyance.

In 1910, the first book attributed to Krishnamurti, *At the Feet of the Master* (Krishnamurti 1974), was published under curious circumstances. The book's author was specified as Alcyone, the name attributed to the soul of Krishnamurti and its many incarnations. Leadbeater became fascinated with tracing the lives of Alcyone, which he reported spanned a period "from 22662 B.C. to A.D. 624" (Tillett 1982: 114). The book, a first-person account of the lessons derived by Krishnamurti/Alcyone from study with Master Kuthumi on the higher planes, remains in print as a "guide for the pupil seeking spiritual and occult development" (Tillett 1982: 137). Authorship of the book became a matter of dispute, however. Because Leadbeater directed the nightly sessions between Krishnamurti and Master Kuthumi and edited all of Krishnamurti's notes – which are no longer extant – "there was no way of measuring to what extent Leadbeater had revised or altered [Krishnamurti's] words" (Tillett 1982: 137). The dispute over authorship of the book, whether Krishnamurti or Leadbeater, persists, with evidence that Krishamurti himself denied authorship in a clear statement to his father (Tillett 1982: 138–9).

Around the turn of the twentieth century the Theosophical movement had begun to decline, but under the formidable leadership of Annie Besant, many

Figure 3 J. Krishnamurti and Annie Besant, c. 1924. Courtesy Krishnamurti Foundation of America.

lodges in Europe, America, and India revived (see Figure 3). As president of the Society, Besant, with the aim of drawing together those who believed in the coming of the World Teacher and were willing to contribute to his mission, initiated several groups within the Society, culminating in 1911 with the creation of the Order of the Star in the East (OSE) and an accompanying journal *The Herald of the Star*, with Krishnamurti as nominal editor.

Following the creation of the OSE, dissension arose among Society members who held that Besant had imposed an occult adventist agenda and messianic opinions about Krishnamurti on members of the Society who were clearly not amenable, as these impositions extended far beyond the three original objectives of the Society (Lutyens 1975: 46). Among some Theosophists, Besant's "proclamation of the World-Teacher [*sic*] and the progressive messianic movement as embodied in the Order of the Star in the East" was a "departure from Theosophy as taught by Madame Blavatsky" and was termed "Neo-Theosophy" (Wessinger 1988: 275–7). Because of these differences between the original aims of the Theosophical Society and those of "Neo-Theosophy," Besant created and maintained an organizational distinction between the Theosophical Society and the OSE. Apart from these disagreements, however, the Society and the OSE were hardly distinguishable, as the same people attended meetings and held high office in both organizations. As a result, "some members, and indeed whole sections of the Society, disagreed, and departed" (Tillett 1982: 138–9). The OSE claimed 43,000 members in its annual report of 1926, two-thirds of whom were also members of the Theosophical Society (Lutyens 1990: 62). In 1927, the OSE was reorganized to reflect the fact that the awaited coming of the World Teacher had changed to reflect, in Besant's words, that "The World Teacher is here" (Lutyens 1990: 67) and was renamed The Order of the Star.

Beginning in 1911 and continuing over the next decade, under the guardianship of Besant and the continued instruction by Leadbeater and several tutors, Krishnamurti studied English, history, mathematics, and sports. Leadbeater personally oversaw Krishnamurti's maturation in his understanding of the Society and its occult teachings (Lutyens 1975: 45–6). As an adept at occult matters, Leadbeater claimed that he was present clairvoyantly during sleep at the initiations of various Theosophical Society members into higher and higher planes of existence, which he reported to each member after waking the next morning. Krishnamurti's progressive initiations on the astral plane were reported in this fashion (Tillett 1982: 129–34). Specifically, Leadbeater reported, Krishnamurti was accepted as a student of Master Kuthumi who vouched for his worthiness and entrusted Leadbeater and Besant to help him on his upward way in the outer world (Tillett 1982: 131). In this way, Krishnamurti's life was planned and directed through instructions from Master Kuthumi, transmitted through Leadbeater.

While Narianiah was living outside the Adyar compound, Krishnamurti and his brother were living inside, near Besant and Leadbeater, and took their meals there. In 1910, Narianiah transferred guardianship of his sons to Besant. In 1911 and extending for several years, a scandal ensued surrounding Leadbeater's impropriety regarding sexual conduct with boys in his charge, including Krishnamurti and Nitya. In 1912, Narianiah complained to the District Judge of Chingleput that his sons were being corrupted through unnatural acts by Leadbeater and sought to annul any grant of guardianship to Besant, who did not keep the boys separate from Leadbeater. Narianiah alleged that he witnessed improper and unnatural acts between Leadbeater and Krishnamurti. Besant fought to retain guardianship. Several court cases ensued, ending with an appeal to the Privy Council in England, which decided in Besant's favor, so that Krishnamurti and Nitya were under the guardianship of Besant until they reached the age of eighteen (Lutyens 1975: 54–84; Tillett 1982: 140–57). Although the facts surrounding Leadbeater's improprieties concerning young boys remain controversial, it appears evident that Leadbeater "had no sexual relationship with Krishnamurti or Nityananda" even though "there were 'irregularities' in Leadbeater's relationships with his closest pupils on other occasions, and Mrs. Besant was aware of this fact, but unwilling, or unable, to take any action" (Tillett 1982: 155).

At the Theosophical Convention at Benares in December 1911, Krishnamurti was to demonstrate the first manifestation of the Lord Maitreya, which Leadbeater felt as a "tremendous power flowing through him [Krishnamurti]," and prompted others in attendance to fall at his feet and weep (Lutyens 1990: 16). The next day, Besant informed the Esoteric Section that "after what they had seen and felt, it was no longer possible to make even a pretence of concealing the fact that Krishna's body had been chosen by the Bodhisattva and was even now being attuned to him" (Lutyens 1990: 16). Following this pivotal event and the conflict over custody of Krishnamurti and his brother, Krishnamurti began to exert some personal independence, but remained largely under the guidance of Besant and the instruction of Society members at Adyar. His independence would grow exponentially with his experiences in the 1920s.

The Process

In 1922 Krishnamurti, now in his twenties, and Nityananda traveled to Sydney, Australia, to attend a Theosophical convention. After deciding to visit the United States on their return to Europe, they were invited to spend time in Ojai, California, near Santa Barbara. The remote valley afforded a location for the brothers to be alone together, and its dry climate was particularly helpful for Nitya's tuberculosis, a growing concern. Krishnamurti was "enchanted with the beauty of the countryside," and Besant later bought the property for the brothers (Jayakar 1986: 46–7). Named Arya Vihara, "the monastery of the noble ones," the property became a permanent home for Krishnamurti throughout his life as well as his place of death (Jayakar 1986: 47).

Beginning in August 1922, at the age of twenty-seven, Krishnamurti "was to be plunged into the intense spiritual awakening that changed the course of his life" (Jayakar 1986: 47). While at Ojai, he underwent an intense, life-altering transition, begun earlier in Holland, that was understood as a profound "transformative event that lasted for months and was to recur to the end of his life" (Lee 2020: 8). This experience, called "the Process," began as formal meditation, but moved on to involve "pain, nausea, hallucination, disembodied voices, and the apparition of religious figures" (Lee 2020: 8). It contained moments of great beauty and clarity offset by periods of physical pain, even agony. He fell unconscious, conversed with nonphysical entities, and spoke from several personas. On occasion he talked as if observing himself and the Process from a distance and referred to himself in third person. In general, the import attributed to the Process was that Krishnamurti's body was being prepared to serve as a receptacle of the higher consciousness of the Lord Maitreya (Lutyens 1975: 165–88) and was similar to a "classic description of arousing of kundalini" (Jayakar 1986: 59).

Krishnamurti's report of his transformation of consciousness is consistent with other reports of mystical nondualism, wherein personality dissolves into communion with all else. In his words,

> On the first day while I was in that state and more conscious of the things around me, I had the first most extraordinary experience. There was a man mending the road; that man was myself; the pickaxe he held was myself; the very stone which he was breaking up was a part of me; the tender blade of grass was my very being, and the tree beside the man was myself. I almost could feel and think like the roadmender and I could feel the wind passing through the tree, and the little ant on the blade of grass I could feel. The birds, the dust, and the very noise were a part of me. Just then there was a car passing by at some distance; I was the driver, the engine, and the tyres; as the car went further away from me, I was going away from myself. I was in everything or rather everything was in me, inanimate and animate, the mountain, the worm and all breathing things. All day long I remained in this happy condition. (Lee 2020: 32)

This description of the result of the Process contains themes that appear in Krishnamurti's teaching throughout his life.[1] Later, in a letter to Besant and Leadbeater, he elaborated, offering other themes of a recurring vision.

> I was supremely happy, for I had seen. Nothing could ever be the same. I have drunk of the clear and pure waters at the source of the fountain of Life and my thirst was appeased. Nevermore could I be thirsty, nevermore could I be in utter darkness. I have seen the Light. I have touched compassion which heals all sorrow and suffering; it is not for myself, but for the world. I have stood on the mountain top and gazed at the mighty Beings. I have seen the glorious and healing Light. The fountain of Truth has been revealed to me and the darkness has been dispersed. Love in all its glory has intoxicated my heart; my heart can never be closed. I have drunk at the fountain of Joy and eternal Beauty. I am God-intoxicated! (Lee 2020: 34)

---

[1] For this reason, Krishnamurti is often referred to as a mystic, meaning that he had attained a heightened self-awareness and expansion of consciousness, even union with the formless, transcendent reality. This Element does not rely on the label of mystic to refer to Krishnamurti the person, although much of the literature cited aligns the goal of his teaching with the aim of achieving mystical awareness.

Accounts of the Process by all witnesses concur that Krishnamurti's awakening constituted a mystery, "a window into a world of great energy, love, and power" (Lee 2020: 15). After the Process was complete – although sporadic incidents recurred for sixty-four years (Lee 2020: 15) – another incident was to prove pivotal to Krishnamurti's relationship to the Society. In 1925, as Nitya's health was jeopardized by influenza in Ojai, Besant and Krishnamurti were assured that the Masters would see that the illness would be overcome, that "Nitya was essential for K's life-mission and therefore he would not be allowed to die" (Lutyens 1975: 219). With this assurance, Krishnamurti left the person dearest to him to travel to India. Yet, during the voyage, he received a telegram of Nitya's death. With this immense loss and its consequent sorrow, "all physical references to the Masters ceased" (Jayakar 1986: 70). From then on, Krishnamurti "seems to have lost all faith in the Masters as presented by Leadbeater, though not in the Lord Maitreya and his own role as the vehicle" (Lutyens 1990: 58). This dissolution of trust in the Masters following Nitya's death and the newfound perspective provided by the Process contributed to Krishnamurti's growing distance from the authority structure of the Theosophical Society and its emphasis on the study and practice of occultism.

From a stance of overwhelming dissatisfaction with the Society, his talks began to emphasize the benefit of self-inquiry in the search for truth, a direction antithetical to the Theosophical structure of that day. Although he did not deny the existence of the Masters, in 1927 Krishnamurti began to say that the Masters and all other gurus are unnecessary, that everyone must find truth for himself. The following year, he told his audience "I hope that you will not listen to anyone, but will listen only to your own intuition, your own understanding, and give a public refusal to those who would be your interpreters" (Lutyens 1983: 14). He began to speak of the liberation of each person and that no one can give liberation to another; each must find it within one's self.

In a rejection of all forms of spiritual authority, he disbanded the Order of the Star in August of 1929 (Jayakar 1986: 78) at the international meeting of the Order in Ommen, Holland, stating,

> I maintain that Truth is a pathless land, and you cannot approach it by any path whatsoever, by any religion, by any sect. ... I do not want to belong to any organization of a spiritual kind. ... If an organization be created for this purpose, it becomes a crutch, a weakness, a bondage, and must cripple the individual, and prevent him from growing, from establishing his uniqueness, which lies in his discovery for himself of that absolute, unconditioned Truth. ... Because I am free, unconditioned, whole ... I desire those who seek to understand me, to be free, not to follow me, not to make out of me a cage. ... You are all depending for your spirituality on someone else. ... No

man from outside can make you free.... You have been accustomed to being told how far you have advanced, what your spiritual status is. How childish! Who but yourself can tell you if you are incorruptible? ... For two years I have been thinking about this slowly, carefully, patiently, and I have now decided to disband the Order, as I happen to be its Head. You can form other organizations and expect someone else. With that I am not concerned, nor with creating new cages, new decorations for those cages. My only concern is to set men absolutely, unconditionally free. (Lutyens 1983: 15)

Dissolution of the Order marked the beginning of Krishnamurti's career as an independent teacher. His writings and addresses to audiences presented an increasingly clear message that scaled back his teaching to the individual, called for rigorous investigation of self, and rejected institutionalized forms of allegiance and belief as necessary for personal liberation. He spurned the "image of himself as a global keystone" involved with addressing the world's problems at large, saying that "my purpose is only to awaken that knowledge, that desire to discover for yourself" (quoted in Vernon 2000: 179). His own role was defined as that of a "lamp, enlightening what was already there but could not be seen" (Vernon 2000: 179).

Leadbeater and other leaders of the Society rejected Krishnamurti's message because it did not include homage to the occult hierarchy, institutions, or ceremonial practices in which these leaders officiated as the Teacher's "self-appointed apostles," even though such homage was contrary to all directives from the Teacher himself (Lutyens 1975: 210–17). Leadbeater also did not agree with the democratic tone of Krishnamurti's message – that his teaching was, according to Leadbeater, "for the average man and not for one 'who has our special advantages'" (Lutyens 1975: 278). Although Besant remained head of the international Theosophical Society until her death in 1933 and expressed sorrow over the split between Krishnamurti and the Society, she nevertheless continued to be his avid supporter, recognizing that his spiritual attainments and vision superseded her own (Wessinger 1988: 296). For his part, Krishnamurti retained an immense gratitude to Besant for her companionship and guardianship, consistently referring to her as Amma (mother) throughout his life, as he had since 1913 (Lutyens 1983: 20).

2 An Independent Teacher (1929–1986)

At the age of thirty-four, Krishnamurti was no longer affiliated with any organization, nor did he claim personal authority to reveal the truth to anyone. 1929 marked the onset of bleak economic times globally, including the stock market collapse and the beginning of the Great Depression. It also signaled a continuing decline in the Theosophical Society's membership. Having enjoyed an influx of members due to the discovery of the World Teacher and

Krishnamurti's charismatic appearances around the world, the Society began to turn in another direction in the late 1920s. The larger organization was in disarray, having suffered a series of disputes, scandals, defections, schisms, and lawsuits involving almost all the leaders – a persistent phenomenon that began with Blavatsky (Santucci 2006: 1114–23). In the years following 1929, the Society lost a third of its membership (Campbell 1980: 130).

It became clear that some had joined the Theosophical Society to be near the World Teacher, so that, with his separation from the Society, they felt comfortable resigning their membership as well. The Society's leadership stood distant from the dissolution of the Order of the Star, maintaining that the Order was only one of many offshoots of the original Society and that the parent organization would not be affected (Vernon 2000: 189). In actuality, a central figure of the organization had divorced himself from its fold and, further, had undermined the legitimacy of its organization and beliefs. When addressing members of the Society, Krishnamurti stated that any organization, including theirs, based on religious hopes is not only irrelevant but also pernicious and encourages hypocrisy and deceit. Yet, he was invited back regularly to speak to meetings of the Theosophical Society while Besant was in charge and maintained an amicable relationship with the Society until his passing (Vernon 2000: 188–90). As Radha Burnier, President of the Theosophical Society in 1995, wrote in that year on the centenary of his birth, "The connection between J. Krishnamurti (Krishnaji as he was affectionately known) and the Theosophical Society was broken, not because he left – as many members believe – but because people were not ready to listen to a profound message given in terms they were not accustomed to hearing" (Burnier 1995: 104).

Krishnamurti's audiences did not suffer such a decline. Financial support for the maintenance and propagation of his teaching shifted dramatically as he rejected the support of the Theosophical Society, disbanded the Order, and ended all financial connections with these organizations. A united core of students, some quite wealthy, were able to assure him a continued lifestyle of comfort. Some individuals left the Theosophical Society to follow the teachings of Krishnamurti; others retained their membership, while maintaining an allegiance to him; still others came upon Krishnamurti's influence afresh, independent of his past, and became committed to the spread of his ideas. The result was a small but significant coterie of committed individuals who were not members of any organization and did not join any movement, yet supported Krishnamurti in several ways (Lutyens 1983: 17–20).

Building on a publishing trust set up before dissolution of the Order, this coterie established foundations in England, India, Europe, South America, and the United States dedicated to furthering Krishnamurti's teaching, creating schools to enact his teaching, sponsoring his personal appearances, and coordinating publication of his talks (Lutyens 1983: 17–20). These foundations continue to collaborate today to fulfill these functions, but, according to Krishnamurti's dictum, without any formal membership.

From 1929 until the outbreak of the Second World War, Krishnamurti traveled widely, consistently addressing the key themes of freedom, awareness, conditioning, love, and fear. During these years, his delivery became more polished, even as his message became more challenging. While he prioritized revolutionary change at the psychological level over social change, at the same time, he refused to support one nationality or one identity over another in a time of accelerating global conflict – both of which stances led to suspicion and criticism in a time of war. As the world confronted the reality of war, his appearances before public audiences grew more strained when he was questioned about his patriotism and national loyalties. Until the end of the war, he withdrew from public life and led a quiet existence in the Ojai Valley, where he gave occasional talks (Lutyens 1983: 54–63).

Krishnamurti never married and was consistent in his warnings that marriage can restrict individual freedom, stultify relationships, serve as a "sanctification of possessiveness," and preclude the possibility of a genuine relationship with another (Vernon 2000: 203). These views are of a piece with Krishnamurti's concern that human love is confused with "pleasure, competition, jealousy, the desire to possess, to hold, to control and to interfere with another's thinking" (Krishnamurti 1969: 80). Although cautious of marriage, his message consistently focused on the importance of relationships among individuals, and he supported lasting commitments in relationships. Moreover, he did not extol the virtues of celibacy and asceticism, which he considered life-denying, artificially suppressive of natural drives, and potentially a source of power that is "separative and will not bring a comprehension of the whole" (Krishnamurti 2014: 51).

For twenty years, Krishnamurti carried on an intimate relationship with Rosalind Rajagopal, one of the few associates who witnessed the transformative events of the Process in Ojai in 1922–1923. In 1927 Rosalind married D. Rajagopalacharya (referred to as Rajagopal), who had known Krishnamurti since 1920, saw to the first publications of his talks, and occupied several roles, finally acting as his administrative and financial chief. Krishnamurti served as a doting father figure for the Rajagopals' only child, a girl named Radha, who was to describe the relationship between her mother and Krishnamurti in print only after his death (Sloss 1991). According to Sloss, the two had a committed sexual relationship based on mutual love and respect, which was not upsetting to Radha's father, Rajagopal. Publication of Sloss's book prompted a reply by Mary Lutyens, one of Krishnamurti's biographers, in which Lutyens affirms that "The physical relationship is not in dispute and should not come as a shock" (Lutyens 1996: 1). Even though Krishnamurti's bond with Rosalind was not contrary to his teachings, the couple chose not to make their liaison public. The reasons for this secrecy have been the subject of conjecture and even derision, but acceptance of Krishnamurti and his message seems to have been little affected (Vernon 2000: 199–204).

From the end of the Second World War in 1945 until his death in 1986, at the age of ninety, Krishnamurti continuously taught his insights to audiences worldwide. These gatherings grew progressively from an exclusive Theosophical orbit to include all sorts of individuals from a host of nations. His appeal to personal inquiry without the aid of any organization, religion, or belief system and his defiance of all organizations as agents of tyranny and self-hypnosis varied little over the decades (Krishnamurti 1954).

Krishnamurti died in his cottage in Ojai in 1986 from pancreatic cancer. Many of his admirers came to see him in his last months but were tactfully asked to leave. Only a few of his closest associates witnessed his last hours. Near the end, he called for a tape recorder to make a final statement, which he had to be assured would not be altered in any way. In short, he said,

> [F]or seventy years that super-energy – no – that immense energy, immense intelligence, has been using this body. I don't think people realize what tremendous energy and intelligence went through this body ... and now the body can't stand any more. You won't find another body like this, or that supreme intelligence, operating in a body for many hundred years. You won't see it again. When he goes, it goes. There is no consciousness left behind of *that* consciousness of *that* state. They'll all pretend or try to imagine they can get into touch with that. Perhaps they will somewhat if they live the teachings. But nobody has done it. Nobody. And so that's that. (Lutyens 1990: 204–6)

According to his wishes, Krishnamurti was cremated in nearby Ventura, California, with no ritual performed and no memorial set up in his honor (Lutyens 1990: 208).

3 The Context: Teacher and Teaching

Locating Krishnamurti's teaching in terms of extant religious or philosophical systems – an exercise he would disdain – demonstrates an alignment with Asian nondual systems of thought that view ignorance as the central problem of humanity and self-realization as the primary spiritual goal of human existence. Conversely, his teaching is not aligned with Western monotheistic and dualistic emphases on salvation and an afterlife. Analogous to Gautama Buddha, Krishnamurti refused to refer to any deity or to any claims for reward or punishment in successive lifetimes. His emphasis on the cause of suffering and the psychological bondage that results from attachment to personal image, identity, and thought is also consistent with Asian, as well as Western esoteric, notions of the perils of conditioning to, and identification with, roles and images. While concentrating on the human condition in the moment, Krishnamurti refused to entertain conjecture about past and future, whether cast in terms of karmic debt, rewards and punishments, *maya* (illusion), or future bliss (Krishnamurti 1954). He never mentioned deities or angels and, once detached from the Theosophical Society, never again taught the reality of the Masters. Although his first book, published under the name Alcyone, was a record of his tutelage by the Tibetan master Kuthumi, Krishnamurti says these were not his words, but rather the words of the Master who taught him (Krishnamurti 1974a). From occasional references to rebirth or reincarnation made relative to his own life, one infers that he did not completely reject Asian cosmologies or ontologies. However, he never included reincarnation as a factor in his diagnosis of, or remedy for, the human condition. Instead, he emphasized individual instantaneous change in the moment, outside of time, and rejected evolutionary change – whether social, cultural, or spiritual – over time. To him, evolutionary change was not only not acceptable but also not possible (Krishnamurti 1970).

Krishnamurti and his teaching are of a piece. He claimed that his teaching derived not from the study of religious or philosophical systems, but rather from a life of developed awareness that yielded an expansion of consciousness, personal freedom, and love. The first subsection that follows addresses the parallels between Krishnamurti's life and his teaching, examining his refusal to identify himself as anyone other than an inquirer and his rejection of spiritual epithets applied to him. The final three subsections discuss themes that emerged in Krishnamurti's life and became central to his teaching: living free from the known; self-inquiry without authority; and developing acute attention and awareness.

Life Experience Becomes a Message

Although Krishnamurti bases his teaching in his life experiences, he does not identify his own experience as a legitimating factor or authority for validation of his message. He was born and raised in a traditional Brahmin Hindu family, yet he does not identify himself as Brahmin, Hindu, or even Indian. Throughout his life he remained strictly vegetarian, did not consume intoxicants, and practiced Hatha Yoga, although he repeatedly said that the reasons for these practices were not to obey any authority, to align himself with any religion, or to follow a prescribed regime. Highly self-disciplined himself, he did not advise anyone else to follow these practices and, in fact, shunned the notion of self-discipline in his teaching. He engaged in inquiry with scholars and teachers in a variety of religious and scientific traditions, yet he did not claim to follow, represent, or transmit any system or codified path. He had extraordinary experiences of illumination, yet he never advocated a search for transcendence or development of occult powers, stating instead that growth of consciousness is more appropriately found in acute awareness of everyday life. Krishnamurti's message, thus, does not rely on the legitimacy of any external source nor his own status. Instead, he attributes his own understanding and the crux of his teaching to rigorous self-inquiry and development of awareness and attention (see Figure 4).

Krishnamurti was particularly disdainful of the effects brought about by identification of an individual in terms of religion, nation, or culture. "When you call yourself an Indian or a Muslim or a Christian or a European, or anything else, you are being violent," he said. "Do you see why it is violent? Because you are separating yourself from the rest of mankind" (Krishnamurti 1969: 51–2). Krishnamurti applied this stricture to his own identity. When confronted by an educated Indian professional and told that his teaching was purely Advaita (nondual) Vedanta – one of the major philosophical schools of Hinduism – Krishnamurti described himself, in third person, by saying:

Figure 4 J. Krishnamurti, 1935. Courtesy Krishnamurti Foundations.

Figure 5 J. Krishnamurti, 1968. Photo by Mark Edwards, courtesy the Krishnamurti Foundation Trust, Ltd.

> He denies the very tradition with which you invest him. He denies that his teaching is the continuity of the ancient teachings. ... Any acceptance of authority is the very denial of truth, as he has insisted that one must be outside all culture, tradition and social morality. ... He totally denies the past, its teachers, its interpreters, its theories and its formulas. (Krishnamurti 1970: 12)

As Krishnamurti became a teacher in his own right, independent of any tradition or organization (see Figure 5), his addresses did not focus on the Brahmanical tradition that had saturated his early years, the complex cosmology left by Blavatsky as the foundation of the Theosophical worldview, or the preoccupations with the occult that inspired Leadbeater and Besant. Instead, he posited that personal transformation derives exclusively from individual self-inquiry and self-observation, absent any accompanying support from organizations, authorities, higher realms, or even fellow seekers.

His teaching does not rely on a complex metaphysics, evolutionary scheme, or belief system as taught by the Theosophical Society. In fact, he doubted the efficacy of any beliefs or doctrine as productive of real change in an individual. Even though the Theosophical Society was a liberal, pan-religious movement founded on the intention to incorporate the highest teachings of all religions in its quest for truth – not restricted by nationality, tradition, or texts – Krishnamurti came to view the Theosophical Society as limited in its perspective and authoritarian in its procedures. That he examined his life independently and critically and came to doubt the utility of the Theosophical Society, even while under its tutelage, illustrates his assertion that sustained personal inquiry and freeing oneself from conditioning can effect real change in an individual. Krishnamurti distinguished his teachings as an inquiry into the human condition, independent of any allegiance or belief as to what constitutes an authority in spiritual matters, including, and perhaps especially, the Theosophical Society.

Nor did he rely on occult or psychic abilities to evoke altered states of consciousness or define the transcendent realm as an ideal to be reached, often considered validation of spiritual achievement. Instead, Krishnamurti stressed the necessity of expanding consciousness through acuity of awareness in everyday life.

Krishnamurti dissociated himself from the public mantle of World Teacher bestowed upon him by Leadbeater and Besant, but, curiously, he never rejected the notion that he was the vehicle of the World Teacher, the Lord Maitreya, who would inspire a new consciousness in humanity (Wessinger 1988: 287; Lutyens 1990: 83). Even when he learned that "a very early Tibetan manuscript contained a prediction that the Lord Maitreya would incarnate in a being with the name Krishnamurti" (Holroyd 1991: 55), Krishnamurti stated that he was skeptical. He seemed to consider the "enigma of his origins and his identity irrelevant to the truth of the teachings" (Holroyd 1991: 55). Krishnamurti's own words attest to his understanding that his selection was providential, but that the expectations and projections contained in the narrative and organizational structures of the Theosophical Society were inconsistent with, if not contradictory to, his interpretation of the role of World Teacher. In a letter to his enduring confidante Lady Emily Lutyens, mother of a major biographer, he wrote:

> You know, mum, I have never denied it [being the World Teacher], I have only said it does not matter who or what I am but that they should examine what I say, which does not mean that I have denied being the W. T. (Lutyens 1990: 83)

In biographer Lutyens's words, "He was never to deny it" (Lutyens 1990: 83). Curiously, Krishnamurti accepted the ontology (and presumably accompanying prophecies) of a World Teacher, who would enter the world to provide insight into the evolution of consciousness, yet declined the public mantle of World Teacher. This paradoxical situation in which he offered a teaching, a message, without seeking recognition of himself as a source of wisdom or authority is the basis for the epithet "non-guru guru" (Balasundaram 2012: 7–8). He was a teacher and guide, and thus, by one interpretation, a guru; but he did not assume the authority usually attributed to a guru, thus, by another interpretation, he was a non-guru. He was quite clear about the role of teacher that he assumed and the role of guru that he rejected:

> I do not demand a thing from you, neither your worship, nor your flattery, nor your insults, nor your gods. I say "this is a fact; take it or leave it." And most of you will leave it, for the obvious reason that you do not find gratification in it. (Krishnamurti 1954: 14)

Several themes that emerged in Krishnamurti's life became foundational to his teaching: freedom from conditioning and the known; self-inquiry without authority; and developing acute attention and awareness. His entire teaching remained centered around these basic processes.

Freedom from the Known

With the stated goal of making all of humanity absolutely, unconditionally free, Krishnamurti invited those who listened to him to observe their inner selves, including the movement and functions of thought. With each audience, Krishnamurti inquired into the basic nature of humanity and emphasized the necessity of becoming aware of one's conditioning, identification with one's position and thought, and the consequent bondage to fear and time.

Participation in psychological thought – that is, activity of the mind attached to a personal identity – inevitably conditions an individual to live in the past, through constructions of thought that constitute knowledge, the known. Individuals live as "second-hand people" (Krishnamurti 1969: 10), meaning that they accept the knowledge derived from their own thought or from some authority, whether text or teacher. As second-hand people, individuals learn to revere knowledge presented through thought and become unable to perceive what is present and observable outside thought, in the moment (Krishnamurti 1999). They live in an illusory world of notions about self, without grasping the truth of self. They are conditioned. They are not free.

Krishnamurti's terminology regarding the known and truth is quite specific. To him, the known is made up of thought and memory transferred from one person to another or constructed in one's mind. The unknown is the extent of one's conditioning that cannot be readily observed by the psyche and certainly not transmitted from one person to another. Without question, many "truths" exist as facts in the collective of society. These truths are termed by Krishnamurti as the known. But the truth of one's conditioning is idiosyncratic to each person and lies outside these collective truths. Thus, the truth that one seeks to find about oneself is not the known, but rather the unknown and must be discovered anew by each person. Further, this truth cannot be apprehended by thought, whether transferred from another or constructed by oneself. What is needed is to be free from the thought and memory of the known to confront the unknown, the truth of oneself, outside thought (Krishnamurti 1969).

What is needed is to escape the tight grip of conditioning and psychological thought to experience freedom in the mind. Instead of finding guidance through imitation of respected authorities or self-hypnosis, one can investigate through self-inquiry the ways in which one is not free (Krishnamurti 1999: 17–18). Understanding one's lack of freedom requires understanding the edifice created by psychological thought, brought about through observation of self in the present moment, without interference from authority, identification, or conditioning, all of which divide the personal psyche and separate individuals from each other (Krishnamurti 1999: 113). To be free one must die to the "known" to discover for oneself truth, which is limitless, unconditioned, and unapproachable by any path whatsoever (Krishnamurti 1969: 9–33).

According to Krishnamurti, awareness of the unknown in oneself requires a whole and immediate shift in the moment – a revolutionary change that cannot be wrought incrementally through progressive steps. This *seeing* of oneself that he envisions brings an awareness of the whole of oneself that allows a new understanding of being to flower, not dependent upon psychological thought, conditioning, or time. With this seeing, an individual is free from identification with any role or position, which distorts observation of the truth of the situation. When one sees oneself in the moment outside conditioning or identification, one discovers another state of consciousness and awareness without limit, another intelligence beyond intellect. But this discovery occurs only through "not knowing," through inquiry into what cannot be known through psychological thought.

When identification as an observer is absent, one can observe without fear, desire, suppression, or denial. A radical transformation occurs "if there is no background, if there is no observer who is the background" (Krishnamurti 1999: 114). In the very process of observing, change occurs. In this way, one can "be a light to oneself" (Krishnamurti 1999: 2).

Krishnamurti teaches that, because all religions and systems of redemption – whether engaged in the goal of salvation, enlightenment, liberation, or self-realization – are the products of thought, they must be rejected as the source of insight into oneself. Any promise derived from a system of thought can only be an illusion, so Krishnamurti refused to delineate a cosmology, any soteriological system, or any tenets of belief. Once, when asked about astrology and reincarnation, Krishnamurti replied: "It is not a matter of belief; belief is never alive – never real. Reincarnation is a fact, but you have to discover it for yourself, in your life, and not from me or a book" (Lee 2016: 70–1).

In essence, Krishnamurti's teaching lacks any trappings of established traditions, including belief systems, cosmologies, status hierarchies, and authority structures. To Krishnamurti, individual transformation in the moment occurs through developed inquiry, sustained attention, and self-examination, processes that resemble a number of spiritual approaches – such as nondual practices, Indigenous spirituality, and esoteric exercises among others – but are identical to none. Attempts to discover resonances between Krishnamurti's teaching and extant systems of thought and practice offer multiple themes, such as observation of the natural world, the unity behind all diversity, and a call for individual responsibility. Yet, these resonances stop short of any resemblance to legitimizing institutions or authoritative sources found in these systems. Rather, the moment of sincere self-observation is the only verification, the only legitimation, of Krishnamurti's ideas that he would sanction.

Self-Inquiry without Authority

Krishnamurti asserts that transfer of knowledge from experts or texts to an individual's memory is not genuine knowledge of self. Just as a professor of Buddhism does not have the consciousness of the Buddha, one cannot study the ideas of others and gain insight into oneself. Such understanding derives from self-inquiry, which alone produces direct, personal perception of the truth of oneself. Whereas ordinary knowledge is gained through the intellect, through *cognition*, real self-knowledge resides at the level of *perception*, which includes intellect and mind, but is a holistic event that includes all senses and the body, unmediated by psychological thought. Perception is a spontaneous *seeing* of oneself, rather than a cognitive process of *thinking about* oneself. Seeing oneself in the moment cannot be shared among individuals, but must be discovered by each person anew (Krishnamurti 1972).

To Krishnamurti, knowledge about oneself gained through perception requires an orderly mind, open inquiry, and intelligence, all of which are destroyed when one depends upon an external authority. Further, making a teacher or a tradition into an authority destroys inquiry and intelligence; direct knowledge about oneself is the only truth that can change consciousness. When one observes oneself sincerely without judgment, one awakens an intelligence and develops an observing consciousness that can perceive how one is conditioned throughout life to identify as a separate individual with memory and past knowledge of one's own. Through inquiry, one sees that what is deemed "one's own" is a congeries of conditioned responses to experiences that have become habitual and with which one identifies. Further inquiry reveals that this conception of oneself – the ego – is borrowed from outside oneself and is thus illusory and riddled with error. The teaching, therefore, is not to study and understand Krishnamurti's perspective but simply to perceive one's own truth in oneself and how one's consciousness operates, an exploration that must be conducted on one's own (Krishnamurti 1954).

One particularly tenacious obstacle to direct perception of the truth of oneself is negative emotions, which Krishnamurti labels disorder. He says that when one sees this disorder directly, the actual seeing itself changes consciousness. Transformation of consciousness is not produced through an exercise of will or through control of one part of self over another part, but rather, through the actual perception of the disorder in oneself. He asks that one become aware of how disorder, whether irrationality, jealousy, fear, or competition, lives in oneself. Using thought to identify, evaluate, accept, or reject disorder will not eradicate disorder because using the mind in the process of identification enhances the negative emotion that is associated with a role. Rather, seeing the disorder in the moment of awareness, independent of thought, changes the situation immediately; disorder gives way to order. With perception of the uselessness, even danger, of fear, greed, ambition, or conflict, these elements of disorder lessen their hold on the psyche and order emerges from disorder. Freedom from the unconscious habitual bondage of conditioning then results in transformation of consciousness (Krishnamurti 1954).

Awareness and Attention

The crux of Krishnamurti's teaching is to discover and then cultivate an attention that opens to an awareness that is pure, empty, and not filled with the contents of the mind. Of primary importance is to gain insight into one's own consciousness through direct perception of one's personal and unique bondage to mechanical and habitual modes of existence. Attending to the nature of the self allows direct observation of how one is bound ceaselessly to thought, to the remnants of memory, and assumptions built on these remnants. To Krishnamurti, the self, by its very nature, is divisive, separating and isolating an individual from others and creating division and disorder in the psyche.

> By the self, I mean the idea, the memory, the conclusion, the experience, the various forms of nameable and unnameable intentions, the conscious endeavour to be or not to be, the accumulated memory of the unconscious, the racial, the group, the individual, the clan, and the whole of it all. ... Experience strengthens the self, because reaction, response to something seen, is experience. (Krishnamurti 1954: 76–7)

Observation of the self can open one to an awareness of how attention is scattered and subject to the whims of any moment. One can see how these bonds eclipse freedom in consciousness. To experience what is going on in one's awareness requires a focused attention to what exists, to see directly the delusions that identification with ego and self produces. This attention must be a direct experience that occurs without effort and striving, both of which engage the ego and the conditioned self[2] and obscure the possibility of direct awareness. To develop an attention and arrive at an awareness that minimizes the dominance of the self requires being "intelligent in an integrated manner ... to be integrally intelligent means to be without the self" (Krishnamurti 1954: 79).

Beyond the conditioned mind, limited by thought and identification, lies a pure awareness that allows real perception, not simply thinking about such a perception. Acute awareness made possible through pure attention provides freedom from one's memory and thought, expanded consciousness, and transformation (Krishnamurti 1969: 29–33).

4 The Religious Life

> The division between the religious life and the world is the very essence of worldliness. ... We are concerned with the totality of life and not a particular part of it which is considered religious in opposition to the rest. So one begins to see that a religious life is concerned with the whole and not with the particular.
>
> (Krishnamurti, quoted in Krishnamurthy 1995: 221–2)

Krishnamurti's views on religion are not those of a sectarian or one who strives to bring religions to a common table for discourse. His stance is more radical than either of these. His famous statements – "Be a light unto yourselves" and "Truth is a pathless land" – point to his mistrust of the institutional and cognitive structures of religion. Contrary to ordinary references to religion, he spoke of the religious life, particularly the need to participate in the religious mind, but he adamantly rejected the notion that any organized religion, ideology, or belief system could transform human lives or society. Because religion to Krishnamurti is a unifying force psychologically and socially, he deemed as religious the establishment of order and wholeness through many venues, including self-inquiry, education, and the discovery of the sacred, all of which lie outside the ordinary understanding of religion.

---

[2] Krishnamurti often used the terms self, ego, and psyche, without specific definitions, to refer to an individual's conditioned makeup, personal image, or conceptualization of themselves. Even though his description of expanded, unconditioned consciousness is identical to Asian notions of the non-personal ultimate – Brahman, Nirvana, or Tao, commonly capitalized as Self – he never used these terms nor did he capitalize the word self. Instead he referred to the "vastness" of unconditioned consciousness and the individual self.

The Problem of Fragmentation

Complexity in modern society has produced division and specialization of roles, with concomitant fragmentation within the human psyche. Each of the fragmented sectors of society is associated with a particular way of seeing reality and of thinking, producing recognizable labels such as the liberal mind, the corporate mind, the philosophical mind, and others. Individuals accept this fragmentation and assume that all of life is not, indeed cannot be, unitary. Krishnamurti challenges these assumptions and asks if there is a mind that can take in and deal with the whole of life, without fragmentation and division, and, thus, without contradiction.

> Life is one, it's not to be departmentalized. We have to be concerned with the whole of man: with his work, with his love, with his conduct, with his health, his death and his God – as well as with the atomic bomb. It's this fragmentation of man that's making him sick. (Krishnamurti 1960, Vol. I: 91)

Is there a way out of this seemingly inevitable compartmentalization and divisiveness, a way that can reintegrate the fragments of personal lives as well as the distinct areas of society? Krishnamurti's affirmative response to this question is that the religious life is the way out (Holroyd 1991).

That which fragments and divides is not religious, according to Krishnamurti. That which brings together and unites is religious, aside from all definitions of the contents or aims of religion (Krishna 1995). Because definitions received from the world go unquestioned, individuals and groups assume that fragmentation and compartmentalization are inevitable. Krishnamurti rejects this assumption and asserts that it is possible to come upon a mind and a society not based on fragmentation and division and their inevitable results – fear, animosity, and violence.

Wholeness and Order

But how does one end the fragmentation? Since a unified mind is unknown, one can begin only by seeing how one actually is, by finding out what creates division in one's inner life. Even without understanding what order, unity, and absence of conflict are, one can observe the division. By watching thought and the movement of thought as they buttress the conditioned self and identity, one can see the reality of fragmentation within self (Krishnamurti 1982a). One can recognize division within oneself and study the sources of that division within consciousness. Krishnamurti insisted that religion occurs only when there is order in life, and he often spoke of "putting one's house in order," a phrase referring to the work that one does in attempting to see the divisions within oneself (Krishna 1995). Until one's house is put in order, one can neither ask fundamental questions nor arrive at truth. Krishnamurti was quite clear in specifying that one cannot put one's house in order by setting oneself against disorder through opposition and conflict between parts of the psyche, but only through the direct perception of disorder.

Seeing oneself without distortion brings order. "In understanding, in looking at disorder, being attentive, aware choicelessly of disorder, order comes naturally, easily, without any effort. ... And such order is necessary" (Krishnamurti 1999: 89). Once brought to awareness, the many elements of disorder – the contradictions, compulsions, opposing desires – of one's mind are transformed into order. To Krishnamurti, order in one's mind is the only entrée to meditation. This order is not a blueprint imposed by society, culture, environment, or obedience. It comes only through the understanding and awareness of the ways in which disorder allows contradictions, oppositions, and violence to exist unnoticed (Krishnamurti 1999).

That state of mind that discovers order can only be found by watching the activity of thought without trying to control or judge its process, both of which bring division and conflict. Watching with a quality of mind that is attentive and silent, without the presence of the conditioned self or "me," brings an awareness that is choiceless. Choiceless awareness, for Krishnamurti, is a particular attention that allows an undistorted perception of what is, "a form of awareness in which there is no choice, a choiceless awareness, all your energy is there" (Krishnamurti 1999: 34). When the mind is not functioning through the screen of identification, thought and memory, it is free to inquire into its limitations, to use all of its energy to observe, rather than to support a constructed image or to consider alternatives. Observation with this quality of attention reveals a situation in its simplest form, without any overlay of language or identification. When a situation is revealed in this way, the problematic nature of the situation resolves and one sees the truth, without distortion or avoidance.

Living with an orderly mind, says Krishnamurti, is living without choice. True freedom does not involve weighing and deciding among alternatives, but rather involves the immediate choiceless action of perception. Choice is a function of a "me," separate from the world, but, in the immediacy of action, there is direct contact between the organism and action so that separation and choice disappear (Jayakar & Patwardan 1981: 79). According to Krishnamurti, one can move toward the choiceless awareness of an orderly mind not by choosing between alternatives but by examining the thought processes that created the alternatives.

Krishnamurti's summons is to use inquiry to examine the problem of disorder in self and to disperse disorder. Rediscovery of order, he suggests, also dissolves the illusion that masks reality, while also clearing the confusion that masks unity. Each experience with moving beyond negative emotions and obsessive thinking, however fleeting, is rediscovery of order that creates a trust in inquiry and provides a transformation. One discovers a beauty in consciousness that bears authentic witness to the workings of the psyche.

In essence, order brings certainty, but this is a certainty not born of thought and not describable. This certainty is intelligence that resides in being, not thinking – in attention, not thought. With awareness, one is free from the known and confronts the unknown. "What has been said in the past [about this state of awareness] may be true, but that truth is not yours" (Krishnamurti 1999: 92). Truth must be found again in each person, for oneself. Each person, individually, must discover this light in themselves and learn independently what the truth is. When one discovers this light in oneself and its choiceless awareness, one comes upon a new consciousness (Krishnamurti 1999).

The traditional Indian story of the rope and the snake (Hindupedia 2024) is apropos Krishnamurti's teaching regarding religion. If a person in a dimly lit room mistakes a rope for a snake and is gripped with fear, then it is only diversionary and comforting to teach the person to cope with the fear. What is really needed is that the person understands the truth of the situation, that the room be lit, and that the person sees that the snake is an illusion. As light illuminates the rope, illusion ends, fear disappears, and the truth is seen. Krishnamurti was unequivocal in his assertion that one cannot light the room for another; one must do it for oneself. This dictum, quite succinctly, is the essence of the religious quest:

> One has to be a light to oneself; this light is the law. There is no other law. All the other laws are made by thought and so are fragmentary and contradictory. To be a light to oneself is not to follow the light of another, however reasonable, logical, historical, and however convincing. You cannot be a light to yourself if you are in the dark shadows of authority, of dogma, of conclusion. (Krishnamurti 1999: 2)

Misconceptions

The religious life, according to Krishnamurti, overcomes several misconceptions that infuse individual lives through conditioning, including assumptions about the nature of religious truth, interreligious conflict, learning from authorities, and the suppression of desire. Religion is the quest for truth and order in consciousness, but religious truth cannot be taught; it must be discovered for oneself (Krishnamurti 1999). Whereas scientific knowledge can be shared and accumulated over generations, religious truth depends upon personal insight that is not the province of knowledge, memory, or transmission from others. Traditional religious structures, both physical and mental, are products of thought in the service of seeking pleasure and avoiding pain. Krishnamurti asks each person to go beyond thought to transcend the goal of seeking comfort. Religious truth is discovered when one investigates inwardly, not with the aim of seeking pleasure or avoiding pain, but with the aim of discovering truth, however unpleasant and discomfiting truth might be. In this sense, learning is more important than enjoyment; living with questions is more important than arriving at answers (Krishnamurti 1984).

To Krishnamurti, there is no difference between interreligious conflict and the conflict between any two groups that are created and maintained through thought and psychological identification. Interreligious conflict depends upon psychological identification with a group or position and will always exist as long as inner division exists (Krishnamurti 1969: 59–63). Religious strife is simply the outer manifestation of inner disorder. He suggests that if one looks sincerely, without attachment, one will see that anything put together by thought and projected onto the world is not real religion. Real religion is not created by thought, but involves looking and listening, without the movement of thought, without memories, without labels, without time, as though for the first time (Krishnamurti 1953: 36–40).

For Krishnamurti, the religious quest is not found outside the self in conventional morality, which invariably includes suppression of desire, foregoing of pleasure, or overcoming of addictions. Rather, the religious quest is an inner journey that yields the *understanding* of desire, pleasure, and addiction, and having these in their proper place. This understanding can appear only in the absence of suppression, rejection, and denial – through direct observation of the conditioning, identification, and inevitable bondage that define the human condition (Krishnamurti 1969: 34–8). Through this understanding one escapes psychological identification with the body, mind, and emotions and finds an unconditioned part of self that knows genuine freedom (Krishnamurti 1954: 86). An unconditioned consciousness that stands outside of and observes a conditioned consciousness and becomes aware of the limitations of identification and attachment is called by Krishnamurti the "religious mind."

The Religious Mind

> The religious mind is a state of mind in which there is no fear and therefore no belief whatsoever but only *what is – what actually is*. . . . In the religious mind there is that state of silence . . . which is not produced by thought but is the outcome of awareness, which is meditation when the meditator is entirely absent.
>
> (Krishnamurti 1969: 119, italics in original)

Krishnamurti took pains to distinguish between the brain, the physical organ of the body that is conditioned by culture and genetics, and the mind, the human capacity that includes thinking and feeling, and much more. For him, only the mind can go beyond conditioned thinking and feeling to include awareness, observation, attention, and insight. Although the mind can also be conditioned, it is possible to participate in an unconditioned mind in which one can observe thought, be aware of the movement of thought, and realize states that are more holistic than thought. The brain operates at the level of thought, accumulating data from the past through memory in a quest for knowledge. The mind, on the other hand, can perceive something higher, something less subjective, something immediate, something outside of the habitual thought processes of the brain (Krishna 1995).

The brain, because of its conditioning, operates through thought and is bound to memory, accumulating only fragmentary and specialized knowledge. Its understanding is partial, and its proclivity is to find answers quickly. Inquiry ends before partiality is overcome. Mind, on the other hand, is not always in quest of the pleasure and satisfaction of knowing or the comfort of inertia that follows gaining knowledge. Instead, the mind is religious in that it seeks truth and lives naturally with questions, not answers. The unconditioned or religious mind asks fundamental questions, which the conditioned brain cannot. The religious mind, free from conditioning, can approach questions from the state of not knowing, allowing inquiry in depth (Krishnamurti 1999).

Moving toward a religious mind is a tricky situation, because there is no ladder of discrete steps to climb to attain the religious mind; the religious mind can be found only through the religious mind. Krishnamurti's famous statement, "The first step is the everlasting step" (Krishnamurti 1969: 91) refers to this process of immediate awareness. One cannot work with fragments to arrive at a holistic perspective; one must end the fragmentation in the moment to enter an awareness that can appreciate unity – and truth (Krishna 1995).

To Krishnamurti, the religious mind, and thus religion, occurs only when there is order in life – the order that brings freedom from fear, from the hurts of childhood, from the pursuit of pleasure, and from sorrow. This vision of religion stands apart from conventional definitions of religion based on belief structures and codified practices. Traditional religion, to the extent that it is created by thought and produces comfort or anxiety through manipulation of thought, inevitably leads to identification with thought. Through identification with thought, conventional religion relies upon imagination, fear, and sentiment. Such an artifice can never experience order (Krishnamurti 1983b). When the mind is clear, unbiased, and unprejudiced, then order can occur, and, through order, real religion, real freedom, and real intelligence appear. Only the religious mind knows real freedom and real intelligence, because only the religious mind transcends the fragmentary and limited knowledge derived from identification with a religion, culture, or group.

The religious mind moves beyond the limitations of thought to a place of nonduality in which the divisions of observer/observed, seer/seen, and controller/controlled cease. Conventional meditation that relies on rituals, symbols, and discipline perpetuates the division and friction that accompany thought and uses the energy of the mind and body to uphold these divisions. Freeing oneself of the need to hold these divisions in place opens a person to the possibility of contact with the summation of all energy so that one can care, watch, and observe with full attention. In the undivided energy of full attention, one participates in virtue, affection, and compassion – hallmarks of the religious mind (Krishna 1995).

Self-Examination as Religion

But what is the right way of looking? A conditioned mind is all that any individual knows, and a conditioned mind can never understand an unconditioned mind or the truth. When the conditioned mind is used, one "thinks about oneself," one is introspective, and one identifies with one's thoughts. Thinking about oneself initiates a train of thought that operates, often in cloying repetition, to justify the identification of self with actions, habits, thoughts, and values. In this process, a personal self is distinguished from others, division occurs, comparisons are made, and judgments ensue. As long as one identifies with the self, its thoughts, and its actions, one is attached, and division exists in the psyche. In Krishnamurti's terms, this is psychological thought, as distinct from ordinary utilitarian thought. An opinion becomes important because one identifies with it, because one appropriates the idea, because one "owns" the idea. This is not the self-examination that he calls for. Krishnamurti points out that an opinion is just a thought that occurs in a brain. Must one be attached to it? If one can stop identification and attachment, division can end within the self, and one can participate in the religious mind (Krishnamurti 1969: 22–6). "Look at your life, examine all conflict, and end all division" (Krishnamurti 1985).

Krishnamurti is a critic of psychological thought. He sees psychological thinking processes as the source of division because this type of thought builds illusions of what one is, justifies these illusions, identifies with them, becomes attached to their survival and acceptance by others, and, finally, fights with others to maintain them. In his view, there is only one way to end this vicious cycle and that is to see the roots of psychological thought, the functions of identification, and the bondage of attachment. Through observation of these processes, consciousness expands beyond the contracted self to include the higher human emotions of love and compassion. Seeing the root of hatred and animosity, or any disorder, for example, without judgment, negation, self-deception, or fear, is psychological freedom. One's house is put in order. This is the real import of religion and the way in which virtue can be based on genuine understanding rather than conditioned learning (Krishna 2023).

Krishnamurti teaches that because one does not observe one's own creation of images of self and others through psychological thought, one grants these images the status of reality and submits to their legitimacy. In essence, one grants authority to the illusions that thought has created and becomes susceptible to the illusions of self-interest that ideologies promote. One then relates psychologically to these biased positions in regular patterns and further validates the illusions created by thought through justifying, legitimizing, and rationalizing these allegiances, which is yet more participation in psychological thought – ad infinitum. At the collective level, justification of thought-created allegiances contributes to tribalism, intergroup strife, and violence. Observation of this stream of causation develops appreciation of the reality of the situation and allows liberation from this system of bondage (Krishnamurti 1969).

Active inquiry into living without psychological thought and identification leads to inquiry into the nature of observation and attention. While identification drains energy, self-observation from a mind that is empty, without memory, brings a focused attention and much energy. The mind can inquire without using a pattern from the past and can observe the biases of thought, brought over from years of conditioning to identities of race, gender, class, or religion. One can observe how division and fragmentation are embedded in these identities and keep the mind bound to the past. Exposed to the light of free attention that is not driven by ego, the mind can approach an intelligence and a perception that sees in the moment the fragmentation in self and moves toward integration and wholeness. Krishnamurti equates the attention of the whole of oneself with the religious mind (Krishnamurti 1969: 119–20).

The ending of fragmentation within oneself does not differ from the ending of fragmentation in social relationships. Both inner and outer are part of the same reality. If one inquires into both, without dogma and presuppositions, one can see the source of fragmentation as well as conflict in all relationships, because consciousness interacts with everything. Krishnamurti notes that sincere observation reveals that conflict exists in all relationships – with people, with nature, with one's body, and even with one's ideas. This conflict is rooted in psychological reactions that stem from identification with a position that confers a sense of ownership or entitlement and ensuing expectations that can be quite unrealistic. Without identification with any religion, concept, or group, one can observe, in Krishnamurti's words, "What is – what actually is" (1969: 119). This means that the truly religious mind simply investigates, without identification with any idea or group, without the goal of justifying identification or image. When identification is present, division and conflict are inevitable and preclude the clear perception necessary for self-examination (Krishna 2023).

Discovery of the Sacred

The religious life, to Krishnamurti, is an inquiry into both the nature of reality and one's responsibility to perceive this reality. As such, the religious life constitutes a movement away from the desacralization of modern society – whether brought about by religious or nonreligious forces – to a re-sacralization of all of life. Alongside nondual philosophies, he assesses the common Western distinction between sacred and profane spheres as a misperception that leaves most of life "un-sacred." As reports of nondual and mystical experience reveal, any objective distinction between sacred and profane spheres is difficult to support, because experiences of transcendence and mystical oneness occur outside conditioning and are felt as sacred, even when they occur in the most mundane settings. Thus, the categorization of a phenomenon as sacred or profane depends upon the state of consciousness, not on the physical setting. When identification and conditioning give way to the religious mind, every happening and every conscious state share the potential to be sacred, according to Krishnamurti.

> The sacred is that which is deathless, timeless, from eternity to eternity, that which has no beginning and no end. You can't find it out, nobody can find it out – it may come when you have discarded all the things that thought has made sacred. (Krishnamurti 1999: 62)

Freedom from the bonds of identification and conditioning provides access to the sacralization of everyday life that cannot be the result of thought, however well cultivated. The religious life is, simply, a re-sacralization of all experience, whether inquiry, education, or everyday life, through a transformed consciousness.

> And that is the only thing that is sacred – not the images, the rituals, the saviors, the gurus, the visions. Only that thing is sacred, which mind has come upon without asking because in itself it is totally empty. Only in that which has emptiness can a new thing take place. (Krishnamurti 1999: 133)

5 Meditation in Everyday Life

Within the overarching project of self-inquiry, Krishnamurti deems meditation as the state of consciousness that includes the awareness and attention necessary for carrying out self-observation, deconditioning, and freedom from the known – hallmarks of the religious life. Meditation includes cultivating an empty mind; overcoming identification with "me" or "mine;" resolving the fragmentation within self into a psychic wholeness, marked by silence and spaciousness; and confronting the new and unknown by letting go of thought and psychological memory.

Meditation versus Meditation Practice

Meditation is generally defined as an effort in which rituals or specific techniques are used to move beyond an ordinary, scattered, and inharmonious state of body, mind, and emotions to a non-ordinary state of stillness, harmony, and expanded perception. As with many spiritual exercises, meditation can be understood as a means to an end, with the end conceived as a temporarily or permanently transformed consciousness. In this view, meditation is usually considered a process set apart from ordinary life – a system of repeating mantras, chanting, saying rosaries, sensing the body, or breathing exercises, and of finding release from the mental disorganization and bodily tension that comprise the routines of daily life. Others do not define meditation as a process set apart, but rather seek to integrate meditation into everyday life without the assistance of specific techniques. Krishnamurti's position on meditation is more radical than either of these positions, as it involves transformation of each moment through awareness, active attention, and inquiry.

> Meditation is not a separate thing from life; it is the very essence of life, the very essence of daily living. To listen to those bells, to hear the laughter of that peasant as he walks by with his wife, to listen to the sound of the bell on the bicycle of the little girl as she passes by; it is the whole of life, and not just a fragment of it, that meditation opens. (Krishnamurti 2002 [1979]: 17)

Throughout Krishnamurti's many commentaries on the state of meditation, he consistently warned against meditation methods, emphasizing that anything practiced mechanically will lead to mechanical results. "One must totally deny all postures, all breathing exercises, all activities of thought" (Krishnamurti 1999: 32). He rejected the notion that one can come to an unconditioned state through any routinized practice or that spontaneous awareness can enter a mind that relies on repetitive patterns (Jones 2015: 656–66). Further, he was suspicious of meditation techniques, however revered, because he considered ego-driven meditation practice damaging to the mind, making it rigid and closed to creativity (Patrik 1995). "A mind made dull by a method cannot possibly be intelligent and free to observe" (Krishnamurti 1972: 92).

To Krishnamurti, meditation is observation or seeing what is in the current moment, without involving any technique or any conceptualization of what is seen. For example, when one observes a tree, one has a direct experience of the tree. "When the observer says, 'that is an oak tree,' that knowledge is the past and that past is the observer" (Krishnamurti 1999: 68). With this cognition, one is no longer in the realm of the present, in meditation, but is in the realm of thought, knowledge, and the past. Following a technique or method for meditation is also a reliance on thought and knowledge as well as an attempt to control and discipline thought. Using a technique or method for meditation is one fragment of thought trying to control another fragment of thought. A part of oneself, imbued with authority derived from thought, seeks to control another part of self that is fragmentary and scattered. However, both parts are oneself, and both parts depend upon thought for their existence. By seeking to control, suppress, or discipline thought through thought itself, one creates division in oneself and uses a great deal of energy to perpetuate this division (Krishnamurti 1999).

For Krishnamurti, true meditation is beyond technique, tradition, or control; it is an all-pervading existential approach to every moment of life.

> Meditation is not something that *you* do. Meditation is a movement into the whole question of our living: how we live, how we behave, whether we have fears, anxieties, sorrows; whether we are everlastingly pursuing pleasure; and whether we have built images about ourselves and about others. (Krishnamurti 1999: 52–3, italics in original)

The assumption that one "does" meditation brings a number of hazards that reinforce both conditioning and identification, the original problems to be surmounted. For example, when one asks how to meditate, "the 'how' implies a method" (Krishnamurti 1972: 93) and an "I" who experiences. Both the method and the identification of self as a meditator bring fresh conditioning, the exact opposite of the liberatory function of meditation. Using a method or meditation practice also creates psychological space between the observer and the observed, and that space creates division and fragmentation within the self, which precludes the possibility of acute perception, which is real meditation. Similarly, if a method is used to escape life or to find refuge from discomfort, a technique can circumvent, even nullify, observation of one's situation. At a deeper level, if there is identification with a practice and a motivation to achieve an end, meditation becomes a tool to reinforce, not transcend, illusion and to buttress the ego (Krishnamurti 1972).

> Real meditation lies beyond any procedures, beyond all effort, and beyond any consideration of "me." Only there can the mind be free from the known and free from psychological memory. Only there can meditation and order exist, so that the mind, which is not of thought, then becomes utterly quiet, silent. (Krishnamurti 1999: 22–3)

Krishnamurti points out that when meditation practice is motivated by a searching mind or the desire to achieve anything – whether peace of mind or exalted states of consciousness – such a practice involves recognition, as one recognizes what one is searching for. "So, in the experience which comes through search in which recognition is involved, there is nothing new, it has already been known" (Krishnamurti 1972: 91). As he summarizes, "Do what you will, the known cannot reach out for the unknown. Meditation is the dying to the known" (2002 [1979]: 48). In this way, even visions of saints and saviors are conditioned because they are recognized, known. There is nothing new in the experience of the vision. To Krishnamurti, real meditation must be a completely new and unanticipated experience with the unknown. Only in meeting the unknown is there freedom.

> Meditation is something that is of daily life. It is your movement of life, and then there is in that movement freedom, order, and out of that flowers great silence. Only when you have come to that point, one finds there is something absolutely sacred. (Krishnamurti 1983a: 32)

Overcoming Conditioning: When the "Me" Is Absent

Thought creates divisions based on imitation, authority, control, comparison, and evaluation – all based on conditioning. Thought, born from memory and what is known, provides images of self, usually situationally dependent, assumed to be valid: one is wounded, hurt, admired, and so on. In seeking to validate to oneself and others the myriad, even conflicting, images constructed by thought, one becomes attached to notions of self. Thought continues to anticipate ways in which an image of self might not be validated psychologically or socially, so that discomforts, anxiety, fear, and pain arise. Thought also generates desire and an impetus to move beyond the present. Rather than fall victim to the many ways in which one's image of self can be undermined, one exerts the action of will to go from present discomfort to amelioration of fears. Yet, operating from the action of will creates even more problems since exerting will creates internal division: both between parts of self and between present and future. Setting intentions for searching, seeking, and desiring goals for some future time sets up psychological fragmentation and the impossibility of living in the present moment. Yet, the psyche continues to divide both attention and energy in the pursuit of finding some wholeness, not in the present moment but in some future moment. One also continues to use thought to rationalize this division and to imagine the realization of what one fears (Krishnamurti 1983a: 69–84).

When a person acts from identification, that is, from having a sense of oneself, a duality is set up between the observer and the observed. As an example, one can internally identify as a meditator who has a fragmented consciousness, but wants to experience wholeness. The meditator assumes that through the force of will, they can attain another state of consciousness. These thoughts and intentions set identity apart from actions, with the assumption that the force of intention can change one's state of consciousness. However, when one observes sincerely, one sees that, rather than an expanded state of consciousness, one has created division and conflict within one's own consciousness. One part of self seeks to control another part. Krishnamurti asks if, unfettered by attachment to an image of self or identification with what is me and mine, one can live without psychological memory (Krishnamurti 1983a: 21).

> Memory is necessary at a certain level, but not at the psychological level. When there is the awareness that cleanses the brain of any accumulation as memory, then the "me" progressing, the "me" achieving, the "me" in conflict, comes to an end because you have put your house in order. (Krishnamurti 1999: 34).

Meditation is the state of attention in which the me is totally absent (Krishnamurti 1999: 65–6). Consequently, no trace of motive, will, or intention is present. The mind is free from fear, the anxieties that accompany attachment to the image of me, and the friction of a mind in conflict with itself. "In meditation, life becomes a total movement, not fragmented and broken up as the 'me' and the 'you'" (Krishnamurti 1999: 68). One needs to see the truth of the situation – "that the controller is the controlled, the experiencer is the experienced, the thinker is the thought. They are not separate entities. If you understand that, then there is no necessity to control" (Krishnamurti 1999: 4). In Krishnamurti's teaching, meditation is not disciplining of thought, reliance on external or internal authority, or control of desire – all of which are common notions of meditation. Instead, "meditation in daily life is a transformation of the mind, a psychological revolution so that we live a daily life – not in theory, not as an ideal, but in every movement of that life – in which there is compassion, love, and the energy to transcend all the pettiness, the narrowness, the shallowness"(Krishnamurti 1999: 8). This revolution brings an active attention and deep stillness derived from a mind that is "young, fresh, innocent" (Krishnamurti 1999: 8).

Finding Wholeness

Meditation is movement out of division in oneself into a wholeness that does not contain psychological identification, desire, or will. In meditation, one gains insight into the whole of oneself, which implies "having no motive, no remembrance, just instant perception of the nature of consciousness" (Krishnamurti 1999: 60). Meditation is also outside of the division that time creates: "there is no tomorrow, psychologically" (Krishnamurti 1999: 55). There is only the active attention of the present moment of awareness. Timeless, deathless, with no beginning and no end, meditation is a new consciousness that cannot evolve over time but must be found in an instantaneous process outside of time.

Meditation for Krishnamurti is not a practice, but an instantaneous, immediate break with conditioning. Movement beyond the fragmentation of conditioning to a sudden, holistic experience is described by Krishnamurti as revolutionary, as distinguished from commonly held descriptions of meditation techniques that are evolutionary and incremental. In revolutionary meditation, the limitations of thought cease, and one enters a state of limitless space, infinity, in which all perception is enhanced. "One learns the art of observing without any distortion, without any motive, without any purpose – just to observe" (Krishnamurti 1979: 193). In this state one can see the conditioned mind and the limitations of thought because perception stands outside these limitations.

In Krishnamurti's view, meditation occurs; it is not achieved (see Figure 6). When meditation occurs, the brain, which habitually accommodates incessant chattering to itself, becomes silent. When the brain is quiet, very still, and not chattering to itself – only then does the religious mind appear (Krishnamurti 1972). In the absence of any notion of "me," one approaches an intelligence beyond intellect that is holistic and outside the boundaries of thought. Action in this state of consciousness can then derive from love and compassion, devoid of egoistic motives (Krishnamurti 1979).

To Krishnamurti, the full attention of meditation is not concentration, which is another form of division in the mind as one exerts effort to exclude certain thoughts to concentrate on one thought. Concentration narrows one's attention and sets up a system of resistance to allow a single train of thought to the exclusion of another. Division, friction, choice, and conflict ensue when one part of the mind is set against another part of the mind. When Krishnamurti speaks of meditation, he points to the awareness that exists beyond duality and the choice, friction, and loss of energy that accompany duality. All of one's energy is available for observation. "Out of meditation comes immense silence, not cultivated silence ... but a silence that is unimaginable. In this silence there is emptiness, an emptiness that is the summation of all energy" (Krishnamurti 1979: 193). Without the activity of thought and definitions of me and not me, all of space is also available. One encounters a vast distance and limitless time, which is the pristine vitality of the brain. Beyond the shackles of thought and its accompanying divisions, outside the structures and "noises" of psychological memory, one meets freedom. Here one encounters not relative but "absolute silence of the mind" and finds wholeness (Krishnamurti 1999: 35).

Figure 6 J. Krishnamurti, 1978. Photo by Michael Mendizza, courtesy the Krishnamurti Foundation of America.

Confronting the New and the Unknown

To Krishnamurti, meditation is inquiry that resides in stillness, silence, emptiness, and not knowing so that the mind is capable of observing. When the mind and brain become extraordinarily quiet, there is no need for a discipline, a teacher, or a system. In fact, reliance on anything outside oneself will negate the possibility of an extraordinarily quiet mind.

The attention of meditation is quiet, but not passive. It is an awareness, a stillness, a seeing without conscious identification as a "seer." It is a listening with total attention, without identification of either observer or observed, since identification invariably brings distortion of the truth of oneself. The possibility exists to be aware of one's conditioning, one's background, one's impulses, and the general disorder of one's mind, without a desire to change, alter, or transform anything. Just as the body experiences proprioception (self-perception) in space, the mind can experience proprioception of thought simply by observing the movement of thought and emotions (Bohm 1996: 75–83). The simple act of observing is what constitutes both the beginning and the end of meditation, so that "the first step is the last step" (Krishnamurti 1999: 87). The import of this situation is that real change, actual transformation, is effected through *seeing* without the distortion of identification, simply seeing, rather than making any effort of will to transform (Krishnamurti 1999: 105).

Krishnamurti's view of meditation is similar to what many nondual teachings refer to as "presence," generally defined as a disciplined attention that engages a harmonious relationship between body, mind, and emotions (de Llosa 2006: x). In essence, one steps outside the usual chaotic stream of thoughts and associations to become a witness to oneself. Seeing oneself is itself transformative in that the unconscious and habitual state of mind steps aside and a clear perception allows a view into the reality of the situation, including one's lack of freedom and one's captivity to fear, negative emotions, and the incessant review of past knowledge of oneself. With freedom from the known, the mind can confront the unknown. Without bondage to the past through thought, the mind can enter the present as an undivided whole. One can experience the sacred "when thought has discovered itself, its right place, without effort, without will. ... Only when the mind is absolutely free and silent does one discover that which is beyond all words, which is timeless ... the vastness of true meditation" (Krishnamurti 1979: 197).

6 Transformation

From Krishnamurti's perspective, inquiry into one's current plight brings realization that a new consciousness is required to find freedom from the bondage of illusions and habitual nature, all created and reinforced by psychological thought. Accordingly, the expanded awareness brought by inquiry is an opening to transformation that can crystallize change.

> Nothing outside will change us, will bring about mutation. What will change us is only our attention, our own awareness of the confusion in which we live, and watching that, remaining with that completely, not trying to change, not trying to do something about it.
> (Krishnamurti 1982b)

A New Consciousness Beyond Psychological Thought and Time

Krishnamurti's teaching points to the need to discover a new consciousness uncluttered by the habitual companions of conditioning, identification, time boundness, and egocentricity. He suggests that one simply look, with sincerity, and *see* how one is "so fragmented, so terribly limited," so that one never perceives unity or has the feeling of wholeness (Krishnamurti 1999: 50). Looking with sincerity calls upon the light in oneself that Krishnamurti and other religious luminaries – such as the Buddha and Jesus – reference. Finding the light within is an all-encompassing existential approach that involves continual inquiry based on cultivating awareness and attentiveness to perceive the reality of oneself, find truth, and open one's consciousness to the unknown. In moving from *thinking* about oneself to *seeing* oneself in the moment, with a "perception that is not of time and thought" (Krishnamurti 1982a: 35), one moves from cognition to perception, from fragmentation to the experience of limitless, timeless reality. An innate spiritual insight inherent in all individuals, this light in oneself becomes a conduit for integrating a nondual state of awareness into everyday life. Such an integration is transformation of one's state of being (Krishnmurti 1999).

In order to extricate oneself from the old consciousness, which identifies with nationality, race, religion, gender, and so on, Krishnamurti advocates bringing the light of attention, the light in oneself, to illuminate exactly how the old consciousness is conditioned and maintained through psychological thought – how thought creates a reality, then proceeds to create an identification with what it perceives to be reality, and continues to connect the personal self with the very edifices that thought has created. Using thought to identify with a self-image that specifies what is me and mine confines existence to psychological time. One cannot be free. A new consciousness, beyond psychological thought and time, is a place of freedom.

To Krishnamurti, the old consciousness of identification and fragmentation exists not only through thought but also through living in time. Just as order cannot be found in the thinking mind, so learning cannot be found in time. Similarly, transformation of consciousness can occur only in the moment; it cannot be built in an incremental way over time, through thought (Krishnamurti 1969). Krishnamurti was convinced that any reliance on time, with its division of the transformative experience into means and ends is fallacious and perpetuates the very divisions in the psyche that need to be overcome.

> We think that changes in ourselves can come about in time, that order in ourselves can be built up little by little, added to day by day. But time doesn't bring order or peace, so we must stop thinking in terms of gradualness. This means that there is no tomorrow for us to be peaceful in. We have to be orderly on [sic] the instant. (Krishnamurti 1969: 72)

Since living in thought ties one to the past, Krishnamurti poses the question of how to approach the possibility of moving beyond the world of manifestation in which everything that is created has both a beginning and an end. "We are asking if there is something beyond all time" (Krishnamurti 1999: 49). Krishnamurti posits that, when "innocent of time," one can have a "feeling of the complete wholeness and unity of life ... that can come only when there is love and compassion" (Krishnamurti 1999: 50). In the absence of thought and time, one approaches infinity and the sacred. One exists outside manifestation and, thus, outside the opposites that thought imposes on manifestation. Krishnamurti's message of nonduality notes that consciousness is not created by the brain and, thus, is not an emergent phenomenon created by a biochemical process. Rather, consciousness is an infinite, fundamental experience, without form or limit, shared with all humanity and faced through direct awareness, which is eternal – without beginning or end (Krishnamurti 1983a: 33–41).

A new consciousness includes real *understanding* that exists only through awareness, beyond thinking; understanding is not a cognitive process bounded by rationality. Understanding brings an experience of a single, indivisible, eternal whole, which is reality. Perception of reality as multiple occurs only because the mind acts as a prism that refracts the whole and makes it into millions of parts. According to Krishnamurti, there is nothing other than an indivisible whole; understanding this reality is access to truth (Krishnamurti 1983a: 37–41).

The truth of ontological unity – the indivisible whole of reality – is realized through self-inquiry, through being a light to oneself. When one is a light to oneself, one is a light to the world, because the world is not separate from oneself. Undistorted, the mind participates in the truth of the sacred, seeing the world as a whole. Love is another name for that whole. "Meditation is having the feeling of the complete wholeness and unity of life ... and that can come only when there is love and compassion" (Krishnamurti 1999: 50). In this way, a new consciousness, a new culture, and a new civilization can be born from awareness and the love and compassion it brings. Living the religious life and meditation provide a possibility for a new consciousness, which includes finding right relationships with each other and ending suffering. Fragmentation is left behind; wholeness is regained. "In the ending there is a new beginning" (Krishnamurti 1983a: 30).

Krishnamurti's understanding of transformation, although described primarily in intrapsychic terms, is part of a perspective that includes biological, social, and cultural alterations, as well as psychological change. Early on, he spoke of a revolution in consciousness, radical transformation, and a mutation of the brain – changes interpreted by some as being only psychological or spiritual. Later it became obvious that Krishnamurti was referring to biological and organic mutation as fact, not only as metaphor. He taught that proper undirected attention can change the physical structure of a habituated, patterned brain and bring about a mind that is free from the distortions of a conditioned brain. He joined with physicist David Bohm in asserting that brain cells can mutate, not only incrementally over time but also in sudden transformations (Krishnamurti & Bohm 2014).

Developments in the biological and cognitive sciences seem to support several of Krishnamurti's points: his insistence on revolutionary, not evolutionary, change; the perennial nature of change in the brain; his imperative for dying to the known in order to free oneself from recursive patterns in the brain; the need for an attention that relates conscious and unconscious processes; and immediate rather than gradual psycho-biological human mutation (Sanat 1999; Malin 2001; Ferrer 2002; van der Kolk 2014; Costandi 2016).

Krishnamurti's emphasis on mutation of the brain aligns with notions of social and cultural transformation. As the conditioned brain demonstrates a closed system of recursive and persistent patterning, mutations in the brain demonstrate freedom from these conceptual systems and a promise of significant change at the social level. Although the onus for transformation resides squarely with the individual in Krishnamurti's teaching, its effects extend to all, expanding the understanding of unity and order to collective levels (Malin 2004; Sabzevary 2008).

"You Are the World"

Krishnamurti's famous statement, "You are the world" (1972), is not metaphorical or poetic language, but rather a literal statement of nondual ontology and epistemology. In his paradigm, the world, the collective, can be reformed only through psychological transformation of individuals; peace in the world is achieved only by finding peace in individual consciousness. Krishnamurti was clear in pointing to the fact that simply valuing and espousing virtue and nonviolence does not mitigate the truth of psychological violence, so that, even as one espouses a virtue, its opposite most likely exists within self. Acute observation of one's psyche confirms the absence of virtue in self and provides evidence of the need for establishing virtue and nonviolence in both self and society. Transformation of both individual and the collective is then possible. Yet, action toward change, however laudable, is not sufficient to provide this groundwork. First, order must appear in the psyche. Love, compassion, virtue, and nonviolence cannot be attained by decision, effort, or actions of any type if the psyche is disordered. These states of consciousness must be grounded in a state of mind. To Krishnamurti, even the subtlest thoughts can keep disorder and violence alive within oneself. One can be virtuous only by finding order in one's own self (Krishnamurti 1969).

> In oneself lies the whole world, and if you know how to look and learn, then the door is there and the key is in your hand. Nobody on earth can give you either that key or the door to open, except yourself. (Krishnamurti 1972: 158)

To Krishnamurti, each individual shares the consciousness of all humanity; the whole of humankind is in each person. Individuals cannot appreciate this fact because individual selves are the products of disorder, conflict, and conditioning. Humanity is divided because individuals are the products of conceptual thinking – a situation exacerbated by ideologies, whether religious or political, which Krishnamurti viewed as forms of bondage (Krishnamurti 1972: 42–4). By observing oneself, one sees an identity with the world, including the hatreds, the fears, the dedication to nationalism, and the rejection or acceptance of religious separatism. Each person has the same fears, hopes, and desires as all other persons. If one can see that one shares the consciousness of all humanity, one can realize the fact of unity with all. Then, and only then, can one touch a different quality of mind that is holistic, ordered, and integral. The mind that understands the truth of existence and the unity of life will not harm itself or others. Aggression, violence, and brutality, both within and outside the self, will cease (Krishnamurti 1972: 166–8). Seeing that one is part of the global system, says Krishnamurti, is a task for each individual to address, because this feat cannot be done at the group, institutional, or national levels. Only a revolutionary transformation of self will ultimately change the world – because the self is changed.

7 Scholarly Encounters

Krishnamurti's teaching has been explored in a range of publications and dissertations, in both the sciences and humanities. This section reviews selected scholarly engagement with his teaching, which places his contributions within the large arcs of theoretical and practical approaches to transformation of consciousness. A number of Asian thinkers and scholars have written appreciative commentaries on his approach to self-transformation (Mehta 1979, 1987), his participation in perennial philosophy (Sanat 1999), his person in the context of Hindu spirituality (Ravindra 1995), and the similarity of his teachings to those of Buddhism (Samdhong with Mendizza 2017). In addition to considering these commentaries on Krishnamurti's life and work offered from Asian spiritual perspectives, various selected records of conversations between Krishnamurti and scientists, philosophers, religion scholars, and educators are examined. The most significant of these is Krishnamurti's collaboration with David Bohm and their work together on inquiries into the nature of thought and meaning. Krishnamurti introduced a type of dialectic dialogue, and later he and Bohm further developed the process of dialogue in groups. This section concludes with scholarly commentaries and critiques of Krishnamurti's radical rejection of any support for individual journeys toward freedom of consciousness followed by a discussion of why Krishnamurti's teaching appears to have been the cause of few transformations.

Dialogues with Scientists, Philosophers, Religion Scholars, and Educators

Krishnamurti's rejection of all methods and techniques for expanding consciousness and his rejection of traditional sources of knowledge would, at first glance, place him outside the methodology and praxis of science. Yet, he espoused the sine qua non of the scientific perspective – namely, persistent and unsentimental inquiry, without concern as to outcome. In Bohm's words,

> Krishnamurti's work is permeated by what may be called the essence of the scientific approach, when this is considered in its very highest and purest form.... [H]e begins from a fact: the nature of our thought processes.... This fact is established through close attention, involving careful listening to the process of consciousness, and observing it assiduously. (Krishnamurti & Bohm 1999: ix)

Contrary to current linguistic associations, Krishnamurti labeled this pursuit of truth through inquiry "the religious mind," which, he says, deals with facts, with what is actually happening in the world outside and the world inside, "a state of mind in which there is no fear and therefore no belief whatsoever, but only *what is – what actually is*" (Krishnamurti 1969: 119, italics in original). To Krishnamurti, only complete attention, without a self-affirming motive or ideological slant, can provide the direct perception needed to "see what is actually happening when we are engaged in the activity of thinking" (Krishnamurti & Bohm 1999: viii). This notion of religious mind in which the spirit of inquiry informs consideration of any issue through sincerity and deep listening was intended as the basis for the dialogues held with scholars over many years.

A wide range of scholars and religious practitioners engaged in dialogue with Krishnamurti, including religious studies professor Allan Anderson (Krishnamurti 1991); physicist David Bohm (Krishnamurti 1979, 1996b; Krishnamurti & Bohm 1986, 1999, 2014; Moody 2011, 2016); writer and philosopher Aldous Huxley (Krishnamurti 1954; Holroyd 1991); Vedanta scholar Swami Venkatesananda (Krishnamurti 1973); and religion scholars Walpola Rahula and Huston Smith (Krishnamurti 1996b). In one illustrative dialogue in 1977, Krishnamurti joins three scientists – Padmanabhan Krishna (b. 1938), Asit Chandmal (1939–2019), and David Bohm (1917–1992) – to examine the "vicious circle in which one is caught" and the clear perception required to move beyond the dominance of the ego, acknowledging that "the fact that the ego is present, prevents that perception" (Krishna 2015: 56). Krishnamurti observed, "to have an insight into consciousness you don't have to have the ending of the ego; you can have an insight into the whole movement of consciousness" (Krishnamurti in Krishna 2015: 59). The four inquirers explored in depth the intricacies of the extremely difficult nature of breaking through this vicious circle into a new consciousness. In the spirit of dialogue, participants came to an understanding of the development of collective thought and shared meaning through sensitivity, attention, perception, and listening, rather than a specific answer to the problem of being surrounded by the vicious circle of ego (Krishna 2015: 55–110).

Scores of videos and transcriptions record dialogues between Krishnamurti and prominent intellectuals, most of which are available online. For Krishnamurti's part, the conversations are "one expression of a far broader interest in the very act of dialogue and its transformative value" (Tubali 2023: 167). We might then pose a corollary question, with Jayakar (1986: 389–90): What was the attraction that representatives of thought systems ensconced in academic and religious institutions had for Krishnamurti – a path that he consistently refused to sanction as an effective means to understanding truth? Philosopher Jacob Needleman speculates that Krishnamurti's aim as he engaged in dialogue with scientists, philosophers, religion scholars and leaders, and educators was to participate in "communication," which is "possible only between people, not between thoughts or images. To communicate with another there must be the common instantaneous movement of something that is quicker [or 'higher'] than thought" (Needleman 1970: 146).

Meetings between Krishnamurti and scholars, although intended to offer mutually informed inquiry and reciprocal critique in the salutary spirit of dialogic inquiry, did not always accomplish this goal. Sessions frequently concluded with one of two outcomes. On the one hand, the exchange ended without establishing a shared vocabulary and agreement between Krishnamurti and a scholar because clarification of concepts and definitions of terms dominated the exchange. Krishnamurti's dialogue with the philosopher Iris Murdoch (1919–1999) is an example of this outcome (Krishnamurti 1996b: 99–128). Murdoch left the exchange frustrated by a lack of conceptual clarity, by Krishnamurti's refusal to conduct discourse according to established parameters of philosophical discourse, and by their disagreement as to a priori assumptions. On the other hand, a scholar can voluntarily enter Krishnamurti's line of thought in an attempt to create an entry to nondual consciousness through a shared experience. Krishnamurti's dialogue with Needleman (Krishnamurti 1973: 21–56) is an example of this outcome. Needleman accepted the definitions and parameters of his dialogue partner's views and gained a novel experience of his partner's teaching.

Tubali's analysis of many recorded dialogues finds that when a scholar subjects Krishnamurti's definitions and train of thought to the prevailing logic of philosophical argument, "all that remains is a sterile discussion, but when one acknowledges the experiential dimension of the conversation, the dialogue itself can operate as a method for mystical nondual realization" (Tubali 2023: 186). In effect, what Krishnamurti rejected "was the relevance of the thinking mind to the field of mystical or religious understanding" (Tubali 2023: 169). He also rejected the utility of thinking *about* consciousness without exploring and observing the immediate operation of thinking in its relationship to consciousness. In sum, those who did not insist that Krishnamurti move outside his unique frame of reference, including his idiosyncratic definitions and assumptions, were able to follow his statements and experienced a glimpse of a non-conceptual truth.

Recordings of these dialogues demonstrate how inquiry and sensitivity can provide an exchange among participants that is informative, even transformative. On the whole, the outcomes of these exchanges rarely provided definitive findings or conclusions, but, more often, validated the process of dialogue for enlivening communication and for providing refreshed and deepened inquiries into the nuances of perennial questions.

Compared to the philosophical and epistemological systems that swirl in our postmodern Western world, Krishnamurti's teaching is unusual, if not unique. Nevertheless, his message contains echoes of traditional perspectives such as perennialism, Western esotericism, Hinduism, and Buddhism, and his perspective signals a unity of psychology and philosophy that presages some current approaches, especially in regard to the study of consciousness (Chalmers 2010; Varela et al. 2016; Penrose et al. 2017; Damasio 2022). Further, his emphasis on self-inquiry resonates with recent transdisciplinary discoveries that extend beyond the boundaries of any single field of study to address holistic concerns that advance the unity of psychological and social liberation (Bohm & Peat 1987; Grof 1993, 1998; Wilber 2001; Bruntrup & Jaskolla 2017; Ferrer 2017; Laszlo 2017; Ricard & Singer 2017; Eisler & Fry 2019; Mathews 2023).

Krishnamurti and David Bohm

Beginning in 1964 and continuing for two decades, Krishnamurti joined with theoretical physicist David Bohm in an exploration of the human condition through a series of conversations (Moody 2016). As unchoreographed and unscripted exchanges between the two, these dialogues are extemporaneous explorations of ordinary, along with esoteric, questions of human existence. They serve as models for a process of coming together in respectful inquiry to examine one's assumptions and logic as well as a source of definitive insights into the human condition (see Figure 7).

Krishnamurti and Bohm agreed that traditional didactic teaching was limited in its provision of freedom of consciousness and sought a way in which truth and insight could be discovered within individuals and small groups. They saw

Figure 7 J. Krishnamurti and David Bohm, 1983. Photo by Mark Edwards, courtesy Krishnamurti Foundation of America.

the value in attempting to reach beyond the consciousness of an individual to an awareness of the unlimited consciousness shared by all humanity. This attempt is the process of dialogue. In his description, Bohm notes that when the brain is quiet and the mind unoccupied, when there is silence, the brain can cease to be encased in its limited realm of egoic cognitive goals and can function as an antenna of sorts to pick up the more subtle levels of reality (Bohm 1996: 84–93). In Bohm's words, attention is a kind of relation between the limited and unlimited fields of thought which arrives, through more and more subtle levels, to a general level of awareness in which "consciousness in one person differs very little from consciousness in another" (Bohm 1996: 93). This core unity can be construed as the referent for Krishnamurti's phrase "you are the world."

Bohm considered Krishnamurti's insight that the observer and the observed cannot be separated relevant to the meaning of quantum theory and "understanding the fundamental laws of matter in general" (Krishnamurti & Bohm 1999: vii). Bohm was also attracted by Krishnamurti's "intense energy with which he listened and by the freedom from self-protective reservations and barriers with which he responded to what [Bohm] had to say" (Krishnamurti & Bohm, 1999: vii). In their collaboration, Krishnamurti and Bohm integrated physics and psychology, space and time, into a call for a new awareness, outside of time and space, in which the energy in a group offers transformation in the moment, both within and across individuals. In other words, a group can come to a creative inquiry, generating revolutionary change, not evolutionary incrementalism (Krishnamurti & Bohm 2014: 445–82). Many forms of transformation were discussed by the two in their years of dialogue, including the assertion by Krishnamurti that awareness and insight can bring about a mutation of brain cells (Krishnamurti & Bohm 2014: 143–74).

After Krishnamurti's death, Bohm went on to write several treatises on thought, memory, dialogue, and his original conception of the nonempirical and omnipresent interconnectedness of the universe, which he called the implicate order (Bohm 1985, 1994, 1996, 2002). Of a piece with Krishnamurti's nondual ontology, the implicate order does not depend upon time or space for its existence, but, rather, is always and everywhere, pervading the fabric of the universe as potential. Bohm's *Thought as a System* (1994), a transcription of a dialogic seminar held in Ojai in November and December 1990 and published after his death in 1992, offers insight into the nature of thought as the source of human conflict as well as the possibility of individual and collective transformation. This and other works – although the product of Bohm's unique transdisciplinary mastery – resonate with Krishnamurti's teaching. Even after Krishnamurti's death, Bohm continued to participate in dialogue sessions at the Krishnamurti Foundation of America in Ojai, California.

The Process of Dialogue

In addition to formal dialogues with scholars and audience members, Krishnamurti and Bohm advocated the process of dialogue in small groups of individuals who sincerely seek to inquire into the human condition. In their view, dialogue in a group is an egalitarian journey toward discovery through the exchange of ideas and observation of self with no expectation of an outcome. The dialogue process, practiced today in all Krishnamurti Foundations, encourages individual inquiry without authority figures or didactic formality as a means to cultivate an attention that can relate the participant to more subtle levels of being, essential to the development of transformation of self and world.

Dialogue sessions are always organized around questions, and participants are encouraged to engage with others in a perpetual state of inquiry, so that initial questions generate further questions. Living with a question and interacting in a state of openness was to Krishnamurti the surest way to learning and growth. As exchange occurs, participants develop a deep state of listening, so that they are not formulating a response during another's verbal contribution, but remain open to what the other is saying. Essential to development of the skill of listening is to set aside all assumptions one has about others, about the question at hand, and about oneself. If assumptions are operative, especially unconsciously, they function as the observer, affecting the one who sees as well as what is seen and heard. To listen without assumptions not only allows another's contribution to be understood more completely but also allows the listener to observe the process of thought in the moment (Bohm 1996: 15–21; 69–72). As Bohm notes, this process of observing the movement of attention in oneself, proprioception of thought, "actually gets to the root of our problems and opens the way to creative transformation" (Bohm 1996: 24).

Dialogue is intended to address the major elements of Krishnamurti's teaching, discussed earlier – where one can discover, through inquiry, a deeper layer of oneself in a place beyond the conditioned mind; where one can apprehend the source of thought, confusion, and contradiction in oneself; and where one can cultivate an intense awareness that goes beyond the imagery and notions of habitual thought. One can observe the very foundation of disorder in oneself, and this discovery in itself produces order. Revolutionary insight, necessary for real change in oneself, is possible. Moreover, mutual exchange with others at a deep level elicits a group awareness, a common consciousness. An impersonal fellowship characterized by egalitarian, mutual, and open participation can emerge. This collaboration, almost completely lacking in the larger society, provides support and context for further observation (Bohm 1996: 84–95). In Bohm's view, dialogue allows the individual and the group to go beyond the inevitable limitations of thought to an unlimited ground of everything, which touches true being. Here in the unlimited resides silence, emptiness, acute awareness, sensitivity, and an awareness of the whole of existence – what Krishnamurti calls meditation.

Traditions, Authorities, and Organizations

As a general rule, spiritual teachings that aim for transformation of consciousness revere teachers and the heritages they represent as guides for learning about mind, consciousness, and transformation. Krishnamurti, however, spurned all claims to authority, whether from established religious traditions or his own teachings.

Buddhism, the teaching that most resembles Krishnamurti's analysis of the human condition and his perspective on transformation, provides an example of a foundational heritage that produced multiple traditions, teachers, and practices that have existed over millennia to provide guidance and support for spiritual seekers. According to its principles, the transformation of consciousness is best approached by taking refuge in the three jewels of the tradition: influence of an exemplar (Buddha), a teaching or tradition (Dharma), and a community of like-minded aspirants (Sangha). As with other spiritual paths, Buddhist tenets are clear that these three influences, while recommended, are not sufficient for the transformation of consciousness, nor do they assure enlightenment, or liberation, for any person.

In contrast, Krishnamurti rejected the utility of any authority for discovery of truth and rejected the mantle of guru, declaring that he was not an authority on transformation. He consistently shunned identification with a particular tradition or any system of techniques, preferring individual self-inquiry and collaborative dialogue to any set of pedagogical principles. When questioned directly about the ways in which his teaching differed from that of the Buddha, Krishnamurti acknowledged that he shared with Buddhist thought emphases on suffering, conflict, personal effort, mindfulness, and inquiry (Rahula 1996: 18–38). But whereas Buddhism offers specific and distinct help to those who are "on the way" to personal liberation, Krishnamurti rejects the model of a progressive, gradual evolution over time and stipulates that even the "mind must be free psychologically of the idea of progress" (Rahula 1996: 23). As Krishnamurti deemed the very notion of spiritual progress over time as unacceptable, he also scorned the precepts, techniques, and disciplines of any path, including Buddhism, with his statement, "there is no how" (Rahula 1996: 30).

Krishnamurti's unqualified denial of the necessity of amassing knowledge of "everything" (Jayakar 1986: 389–90) sets his teaching apart from the practices of most spiritual traditions, even the most severe. Further, he offers a seeker fewer sources of support than the most austere of eremitic orders that live in solitude and require absolute silence. Even these movements have adepts that are consulted for guidance, on occasion. Other groups that work toward transformation or mystical states, such as Zen or Sufism, gather themselves around organizations that include leaders, study of principles, and communal practices (Landau 2019: 39, 47). Further, from the time of Pythagoras (6th century BCE) to the present, esoteric schools – which espouse the goals of personal transformation parallel to Krishnamurti – that revere a founder, study a teaching, and work together in a community, consider these elements not only beneficial but also essential to praxis.

In his refusal to accept the utility of any established tradition, assistance from self-realized adepts, or participation in a like-minded community, Krishnamurti represents a radical departure from other spiritual paths – a departure that requires elaboration. The tenet that each person must do the inner work required for transformation of self is near-universally accepted in Asian and esoteric religions. In this regard, Krishnamurti's teaching is consistent with those spiritual paths. Without question, no external agent can do an individual's own inner work; each person must find the truth for oneself. But his abjuration of any help, even from adepts in the journey of transformation and others who strive to create a network of support for all aspirants, is radical (Krishnamurti 1971) and extreme. "I maintain that no organization can lead man to spirituality" (Krishnamurti 1996a: 2).

Without question, some organizations can be coercive, deaden one's search for truth, and strengthen the grip of ego (Trungpa 1987: 121–37). It also seems to be the case, however, that no single individual alone, or precious few, can find the freedom of consciousness that Krishnamurti calls for without assistance. He maintains, "You see how absurd is the whole structure that you have built, looking for external help, depending on others for your comfort, for your happiness, for your strength. These can only be found within yourselves" (Krishnamurti 1996a: 6). He spoke these words on the occasion of the dissolution of the Order of the Star to assembled members; he concluded that few, if any, of the members of the Order had attained truth as the proof that "the Order did not yield the result for which it was created." He was referring to the "attainment of Truth," however, "as the only criterion of success" (Landau 2019: 34). That the Order fostered dependence on itself through its hope for a messiah to reveal truth is unquestioned. What remains at issue, unaddressed by Krishnamurti, is why he would use this example as characteristic of all organizations and why nothing short of complete attainment of truth would qualify as a criterion for success.

While Krishnamurti claimed to be independent of any tradition or authority, he also shunned conflict and did not set himself against any tradition. His diagnosis of the ills of the mind, thought, and ego, as well as his suggestion to follow self-inquiry into the depths of the psyche, do not contradict the nondual teachings of Buddhism, the Upanishads, or esoteric teachers of any age. The distinction that sets him apart from, but not in opposition to, these traditions is his insistence on a radically individualistic way to liberation and an uncompromising emphasis on attaining the complete freedom of nondual consciousness instantly, without a gradual progression or assistance from an adept.

Krishnamurti has been criticized because he rebuffs any method or practice that an individual, through sincere inquiry, might use for self-observation or to assist others in a community of seekers (Landau 2019: 49–50). Although he did not advocate any form of assistance in the search for truth, Krishnamurti nevertheless joined with Bohm in promoting the process of dialogue to create a shared energetic field or "common consciousness," a non-observable entity that forms when an impersonal fellowship coheres to shape "one mind" through calling into question personal assumptions, opinions, and identification (Bohm 1996: 32–4). This process functions as a help for all engaged participants, even though such support does not guarantee complete freedom or transformation. In Bohm's words, "Truth does not emerge from opinions; it must emerge from something else – perhaps from a more free movement of the tacit mind" (Bohm 1996: 35). When Krishnamurti joined Bohm in mutual inquiry through dialogue, they advanced the process as a template for deep listening and deconditioning in the moment. Thus, through a decades-long career of expressing his teaching as collaborative inquiry through the meeting of minds, Krishnamurti at least partially contradicts his own categorical tenet.

Another criticism leveled against Krishnamurti is his apparent fostering of radical individualism, that is, "concentrating too much on ourselves and our own 'advancement'" so that self-love is fortified, contrary to his stated intentions (Benjamin 1971: 163). Krishnamurti's insistence on unaided, instantaneous, and categorical transformation as the "only revolution" is a goal that is extremely difficult to achieve, if not beyond the reach of most spiritual aspirants. Nevertheless, self-inquiry, while it must be accomplished within each individual alone, can be supported and guided by suggestions as to how to inquire, how to observe, and how to confront one's self – suggestions that are part of the transmission of Krishnamurti's teaching itself. Another criticism centers on Krishnamurti's emphasis on meditation, choiceless awareness, and complete freedom as equal to the transformed condition itself, because an exclusive focus on the goal of truth, without consideration of any accompanying conditions, ignores any regard of possible means to that end. In Landau's words, "Because he focuses on the enlightened condition itself, and not on the alleged means to achieving it, he seems to relate only to what is really essential and important, free of any ... barriers to realizing it" (2019: 36). Similarly, Krishnamurti's notion that, "insofar as realizing Truth is concerned, using means disrupts rather than helps to achieve what the means are intended for," sets up an unrealistic, perhaps impossible, goal, according to Landau (2019: 37). These examples of comments are representative of challenges to Krishnamurti. Given these considerations, Landau and others (Rahula 1996; Smith 1996; Weber 1996; Tubali 2023: 251–3) discern in Krishnamurti's teaching a misplaced emphasis on the instantaneous and complete experience of truth as the only worthwhile goal, whereas they argue that making an effort and achieving even a momentary freedom of mind also merit notice and appreciation.

Part of Krishnamurti's complaint against organized efforts toward spiritual growth is his rejection of any technique or practice in favor of rigorous inquiry within self. While many would agree that dependence upon a guru or authority, identification with an organization, and repetitive practices may preclude free inquiry in the mind and reinforce accepting a state that stops short of the goal of realizing truth, can this judgment be made against all practices at all times? Landau counters Krishnamurti's assumptions on all of these points. "That Truth or enlightenment, cannot be achieved through any technique is ... empirically false. Many mystical movements regularly employ techniques, including meditation, recitation ... and for many generations, these and similar techniques have helped some of their practitioners to near the condition Krishnamurti talks about" (2019: 37–8). A final critique from Landau explains that, given what appears to be ample realistic evidence of the success, however incremental, of institutionalized paths to expanded consciousness, Krishnamurti's argument to the contrary stands out as speculative and empirically false (2019: 41–3). "If it is clear that some of those who employ techniques and develop spiritually within institutional organization do, in fact, succeed in realizing Truth, speculative arguments [meaning without empirical support] to the contrary become ... irrelevant even if they are very difficult to criticize" (Landau 2019: 43).

Another analysis reports on research into consciousness in the context of the study of mysticism, with only a passing note on Krishnamurti. In this examination, spiritual traditions can be seen as vehicles for the experience of subtle worlds and spiritual ultimates, so that "spiritual inquiry becomes a journey beyond any pregiven goal, an endless exploration and disclosure of the inexhaustible possibilities of an always undetermined mystery" (Ferrer 2017: 197) – a theoretical tone with which Krishnamurti would resonate. Yet, Krishnamurti's denial of any path, tradition, or vehicle toward some participation in the mystery opposes the specifics of psychologist Jorge Ferrer's observation, although his teaching is consistent with the sense of an undetermined outcome. Thus, Ferrer's concluding statement, "Krishnamurti notwithstanding, spiritual truth is not a pathless land, but an infinitely creative adventure" (Ferrer 2017: 197), read carefully, demonstrates that the crux of the difference between Krishnamurti and this scholar is a matter of emphasis, not substance, as both emphasize the participatory and open-ended nature of confronting the unknown in search of expanded consciousness.

The commentators and critics cited in this section agree that Krishnamurti's refusal to consider incremental progression toward the goal of freedom of consciousness and his denial of the possibility of support from any external agent to be a step too far. They identify exceptions to Krishnamurti's categorical statements, cite evidence of evolutionary progress – which he rejects – and provide examples of how his own writings have been inspirational, that is, have served as a means for transformative change. If his message could be qualified to acknowledge that there are varying stages, varying times, and varying modalities of achieving freedom and transformation, these contradictions might be resolved. Without these qualifications, however, his definition of the realization of truth is difficult to conceptualize and almost impossible to achieve. In this way, his teaching is difficult to transmit, a difficulty that diminishes if not defeats Krishnamurti's attested goal to "set men unconditionally free" and points to a second critique of his teaching – the lack of comprehension and embodiment of the teaching by others.

Adherents' Lack of Understanding of the Teaching

Nine days before his death, Krishnamurti spoke of his conviction that all adherents lacked understanding of his consciousness, stating unequivocally that no one had come in touch with the universal consciousness that he knew (Lutyens 1990: 206). Why did Krishnamurti feel, after sixty years of personal dissemination to thousands of audiences, that his teaching evoked so little transformation in response? In one commentator's estimation, Krishnamurti imagined the impossible, that is, transformation without the aid of authority, organization, or practices, based on "excessive," "unrealistic," "overly rigid," and "unrealistic" standards (Landau 2019: 50). Perhaps in these expectations, he envisioned a possibility of individual free inquiry greater than is warranted, given the depravity of the human condition. Perhaps conditioning, identification, and attachment are strong enough in the majority of people to prevent a "state in which the self is absent" so that the ego with its selfish impulses cannot release itself from the memories and neuroses that block freedom in consciousness (Weber 1996: 228–32). Referring to himself at least, Krishnamurti counters, "I say if *one* can do it, everybody can do it" (Weber 1996: 233).

As noted, the exchange between Krishnamurti and three scientists, Chandmal, Krishna, and Bohm, revealed their shared conviction that there was a total lack of understanding and transformation among the many, including those present, who gave serious attention to Krishnamurti and his teaching (Krishna 2015: 55–110). The problem under consideration, according to Krishna, was "your talking to people and your leading the life you are living, both of which should transform people, but it is not happening" (Krishna 2015: 92); in fact, "not a single person has done it" (Krishna 2015: 95). Dialogue among the scientists produced a consensus that defined Krishnamurti as being "in a field," while those who listen to him "have benefitted within the field" (Krishna 2015: 96), even though no one claimed to have attained total freedom or radical transformation. In effect, this dialogue considered the difficulty of discerning if anyone had discovered the state of consciousness that Krishnamurti describes, "To be a real revolutionary requires a complete change of heart and mind, and how few want to free themselves" (Jayakar 1986: 255–6). If proof of the validity of Krishnamurti's message is effected by acknowledged revolutionary change among serious adherents, then the case for its validity is not made. If, however, more modest goals, such as self-reports of expanded awareness, participation in genuine inquiry, and sincere self-observation, are considered, Krishnamurti's message was meaningful and effective to hosts of individuals. In particular, because of Krishnamurti's teaching, some have indeed benefitted from participating in the field generated by Krishnamurti, in that they say that they understand to some extent the extreme inner poverty of their conditioned lives and their habituated and unconscious efforts to hide this poverty from the light of self-observation and inquiry.

The Buddhist scholar Samdhong Rinpoche summarizes the differences between the Buddha's approach to teaching and that of Krishnamurti. It is worth quoting at length:

> When Buddha teaches people, he comes down to the level of the listener, whereas Krishnaji doesn't come down to the level of the listener; he always speaks from his level. The Buddha deals with two levels: namely the relative and the absolute. When Buddha speaks of the absolute, I personally do not find any difference with Krishnaji's teachings or the Buddha's teaching of absolute truth.
>
> When Buddha speaks of relative truth, he always compromises with the acceptance and notions and thoughts of people with whom he is speaking, but Krishnaji never compromises or accepts the conditions of the levels of his listeners.
>
> The other difference between them has to do with the preparation of the listeners. Krishnamurti is silent or doesn't speak about preparation, whereas the Buddha dealt a great deal with preparation of the person to reach the level of transformation. (Samdhong with Mendizza 2017: 16)

Samdhong Rinpoche's analysis demonstrates both the problem with Krishnamurti's rejection of any means or preparation for transformation and the absence of understanding among adherents (see Figure 8). That is, Krishnamurti's inability or unwillingness to meet his listeners at their level of understanding compromises both the reception of his message and the dissemination of his teaching. Those who take Krishnamurti seriously may well find it difficult to believe the truth – as he teaches – that primordial intelligence is operating all the time and that they must simply see this fact. Conditioning to gradual evolution predominates in current narratives of nondual and mystical practices (Suzuki 1970; Ferrer 2002, 2017; Bourgeault 2016, 2020) so that a practical trajectory, often called a journey to enlightened mind, appears feasible if difficult, whereas revolutionary and instantaneous change appears almost impossible, especially without institutional or personal support.

8 Education as Religion

Despite his refusal to institutionalize a movement, Krishnamurti did cooperate in the establishment of several foundations in those countries where his teachings received the most response and to which he regularly returned in his annual rounds of talks. The foundations are not organizations with defined memberships, but rather are service organizations that facilitated his travel, arranged for his public appearances, and continue to publish transcripts of his talks and dialogues. Today,

Figure 8 J. Krishnamurti with Samdhong Rinpoche, date unknown. Photo by Asit Chandal, courtesy Krishnamurti Foundation of America.

the Krishnamurti Educational Centre of Canada, Krishnamurti Foundation Trust United Kingdom, Krishnamurti Foundation India, Fundacion Krishnamurti Latinoamericana in Spain, and Krishnamurti Foundation of America in the United States see to the publication of his writings, sponsor regular dialogue groups, and hold gatherings for study of the teachings.

As Krishnamurti intended, however, the foundations are not religious groups that individuals join, but are rather organizations that sponsor retreats, gatherings, schools, and libraries. They serve as sites for collaboration around inquiry, dialogue with others, and dissemination of Krishnamurti's teachings. Located in Ojai, California, the Krishnamurti Foundation of America maintains a website (www.kfa.org or www.jkrishnamurti.org) that includes a directory of Krishnamurti organizations and schools.

To Krishnamurti, conventional education is part of the reason that one does not know the religious life. Educational institutions and pedagogy have dulled individuals' minds and taught them to accept and make accommodation to a world of great division and sorrow.

> Education should not encourage the individual to conform to society or to be negatively harmonious with it, but help him to discover the true values which come with unbiased investigation and self-awareness. When there is no self-knowledge, self-expression becomes self-assertion, with all its aggressive and ambitious conflicts. Education should awaken the capacity to be self-

aware and not merely indulge in gratifying self-expression. (Krishnamurti 1953: 15)

According to Krishnamurti, to understand life is to understand oneself, which is both the beginning and the end of education (Krishnamurti 1953; Forbes 1995). The aim of education is an integrated mind, characterized by a sense of wonder, an awareness of beauty, and an appreciation of joy in life. An integrated mind and the sensitivity that accompanies it cannot exist in the presence of fear. Thus, traditional educational systems that employ fear and intimidation as motivating factors for learning are, in fact, ensuring that a child's innate sensitivity and appreciation of joy are diminished, if not extinguished. Fear inevitably destroys the vitality of the child, creates fragmentation and conflict, and results in a fragmented self, a segmented consciousness, and a competitive society (Krishnamurti 1953: 57–9). "Education, in the true sense, is the understanding of oneself, for it is in each one of us that the whole of existence is gathered" (Krishnamurti 1953: 17).

Throughout his life Krishnamurti retained an avid interest in educational reform, especially for primary and secondary levels, derived from his views on the deleterious effects of conditioning and identification on consciousness and the need for absolute freedom of mind. He founded schools in India, the United States, and the United Kingdom with a mission to provide a new definition and practice of education, free from the authoritarian and oppressive structures prevalent in most educational institutions.

Krishnamurti often explained his views on the errors of traditional educational institutions and his insights into alternative approaches to instruction. Each tract (1953, 1974b, 2015) points to the need to broaden conventional visions of human needs and capacities as well as to develop the whole individual in an atmosphere of security, freedom, trust, and affection, the attainment of which promotes sensitivity in educators as well as students. Krishnamurti maintains that implementation of his views on educational reform can foster development of a new consciousness on a global scale.

In his view, the major problems with conventional education stem from its chief interest in providing security, success, and comfort through conformity to the norms of society. Striving for security and success are superficial goals, according to Krishnamurti, that are ultimately unattainable, as these goals shift perpetually. The drive toward conformity supplants a search for truth with a relentless pursuit of desires and inevitably leads to mediocrity in all fields. Conformity in educational institutions is a particular challenge to creativity, as it "makes independent thinking extremely difficult" (Krishnamurti 1953: 9). Further problems arise when educators rank achievement and performance, which reinforces competition and fear and, in the process, dulls both heart and mind. What is needed is an integrated outlook on the whole of life that includes a comprehension of self as "total process" and integrates the many parts of the psyche (Krishnamurti 1953: 12), so that education becomes a force for deconditioning (Krishnamurti 2015: 20–37). This search for psychological integration is best approached through an "efficiency inspired by love, which goes far beyond and is much greater than the efficiency of ambition" (Krishnamurti 1953: 13).

> Education is not merely acquiring knowledge, gathering and correlating facts; it is to see the significance of life as a whole. But the whole cannot be approached through the part – which is what governments, organized religions and authoritarian parties are attempting to do. (Krishnamurti 1953: 14)

Absent a drive to conformity and identification with social roles, education can cultivate human beings who use free, unbiased inquiry into self to discover their own intelligence, the significance of life, and real values. As education functions today, individuals are reinforced for being "subservient, mechanical, and deeply thoughtless," creating collective problems of conflict, violence, fear, and anxiety (Krishnamurti 1953: 14–15).

Rather than rely on the educational apparatus to change individuals, Krishnamurti maintains that the individual is of first importance, not the system. "As long as the individual does not understand the total process of himself, no system ... can bring order and peace to the world" (Krishnamurti 1953: 16). The understanding that comes only through self-knowledge of one's complete psychology cannot be cultivated, he asserts, through instilling external ideals, blueprints, or utopian ideologies that produce only mechanical, subservient minds that are conditioned, even coerced, to function as inauthentic, fragmented human beings. Even worse, the classification of children by temperament, demographics, or aptitude reinforces notions of distinction and difference, so that children learn to categorize and judge self and others according to criteria imposed from outside themselves. They are taught to live as "second-hand human beings," who live in "the prison of knowledge" of what they have been told, with nothing new, creative, or original in them (Krishnamurti 2015: 6).

To Krishnamurti, "the educator needs educating. ... To educate the educator is far more difficult than to educate the child because the educator is already set, fixed. ... So a teacher must be beyond the limits of society and its demands, so as to be able to create a new culture, a new structure, a new civilization" (Balasundaram 2012: 12–13). To be an educator is to study a child, to "be alert, watchful, self-aware, [which] demands far greater intelligence and affection than to encourage him to follow an ideal" (Krishnamurti 1953: 24). To cultivate obedience to any ideal excludes love and perpetuates the conditioning of the educator as well as the conditioning of the child (Krishnamurti 1953: 26–7). Thus, educators need to understand themselves and not rely on their own "knowledge," which itself is derived from conditioning to beliefs or ideologies. By not viewing a child through a derived ideal, the educator can operate through love to observe and study the uniqueness of the child. Right education, then, requires that the educator encourage each child to find the psychological freedom that supports a student's observation and awareness of his own conditioning. Practices used in typical educational environments, including reward, punishment, discipline, obedience to authority, and thoughtless acceptance of belief structures, stifle the growth of personal awareness and freedom of expression in the child (Krishnamurti 1953: 31–8).

Krishnamurti points to the need for every individual, whether educator or student, to develop an understanding of relationship, which serves as a "mirror in which the self and all its activities can be seen; only when the ways of the self are understood in the reactions of relationship [is there] creative release from the self" (Krishnamurti 1953: 54). Right education, then, encourages self-exploration without the specter of authority, whether derived from tradition or a teacher, so that freedom can flourish and fear of failure does not arise. Fear is a pervasive problem that arises from both conscious and unconscious sources and can be eliminated only through self-understanding and awareness, not discipline and threat (Krishnamurti 1953: 57–9).

Integral to Krishnamurti's critique of conventional education is its consistent fragmentation of self, particularly the separation of intellect from feeling and body awareness, present in almost all educational venues. This imbalanced emphasis on intellect affords a distorted view of life and a consequent disharmony in the whole psyche. With love and right thinking, according to Krishnamurti, a child, or anyone, can observe the truth of self – its conflicts, contradictions, and pettiness – without fear. Only then can the conflict, competition, and hatred, derived from the collective and assumed to be inevitable, diminish. Education can teach *how* to think, not *what* to think (Krishnamurti 1953: 65–77).

Aligned with this perspective on right education, Krishnamurti outlines characteristics of a school that contributes to integrated individuals – both students and faculty. "Nothing of fundamental value can be accomplished through mass instruction, but only through the careful study and understanding of the difficulties, tendencies, and capacities of each child" (Krishnamurti 1953: 85). Just as the administration of a school should not be carried out by a dominant authority, so faculty should not be considered authorities for students. The milieu should be infused by an atmosphere of freedom, intelligence, co-operation, and affection, so that students and faculty inquire together. If direction is needed, students are "guided" gently by teachers who join students in dedication to creative understanding and free inquiry (Krishnamurti 1953: 88–97). In essence, a proper school functions to instruct educators and parents, as well as students, so that all come to see "that self-knowledge alone, and not the dogmas and rituals of organized religion, can bring about a tranquil mind; and that creation, truth, God, comes into being only when the 'me' and the 'mine' are transcended" (Krishnamurti 1953: 113).

Unconditioning and Education (Krishnamurti 2015) reports conversations held in 1974 and 1975 among Krishnamurti, parents, and teachers concerning the necessity for a radical approach to schooling. Their collaborative attempt to create an exemplary school in Ojai, California, resulted in the establishment of Oak Grove School in 1976. The dialogues set out Krishnamurti's vision for overcoming the limitations of traditional methods of education which, he insisted, instill in most children insecurity, fear, conformity, and adaptation to authoritarian structures. The dialogues examine the hazards of knowledge-based approaches that exclude self-inquiry, narrow creativity, and circumvent development of consciousness. The dialogues also investigate relationships among students and faculty, with a view toward establishing an educational model that emphasizes providing individual freedom in collaborative inquiry and developing the art of listening.

> The whole movement of inquiry into knowledge, into oneself, into the possibility of something beyond knowledge, brings about naturally a psychological revolution, and from this comes, inevitably, a totally different order in human relationships, which is society. The intelligent understanding of all this can bring about a profound change in the consciousness of mankind. (Krishnamurti 2015: xi)

Mark Lee, a longtime colleague of Krishnamurti, describes the extensive preparation that went into creation of the Oak Grove School, including topics as diverse as research into models of alternative education, suggested architectural features, and the nature of convocations for students (2016: 116–233). In each deliberative session, Krishnamurti was an avid participant, inquiring with others as to how the Ojai school would fulfill the intention to "educate religiously, for a religious life beyond schooling" (Lee 2016: 129). Even though a consistent philosophy guides Krishnamurti's vision, he also maintained that:

> Each school should be different from the others, not just imitate; so that it is a creative thing. Brockwood [in England] is entirely different from the Indian schools; and we want this school in Ojai to be entirely different from the

others. ... They all are international, non-authoritarian, non-hierarchical, not the principal first and then the students ... but all of us are creating this [anew]. (Krishnamurti 2015: xix)

Implicit in Krishnamurti's views on education is his intention to affect the state of the world through transformation of individual consciousness. Calling for a radical approach to education and founding schools are integral to his attempts to foster an environment for growth of consciousness. "Until we change fundamentally there can be neither right education nor a peaceful world" (Krishnamurti 1953: 81).

9 Krishnamurti's Legacy

Krishnamurti addresses the problems of every human being, regardless of nationality, religion, class, age, or psychology. He locates the cause of human suffering, social division, and conflict in the social conditioning and identification with ego that lie within each person. The solution to these problems and their causes, he finds, is through acute self-observation in which the mind is completely transformed.

According to Krishnamurti, the process of transformation is both radically individualistic and without a path. He has no use for the customary structures of conventional society that sustain ignorance of the true nature of the human condition. In fact, institutional structures, whether cognitive or social, are a major problem, in his eyes. Individuals learn from these structures only agreed upon, and thus derived, definitions of who they are, individually and collectively, but never learn, really learn, about themselves firsthand. Through genetic conditioning, social programming, and continuous reinforcement, individuals mistakenly, but inevitably, identify as autonomous independent agents of action or as members of groups. All identification is a fiction, an illusion, and an impediment to awakening, according to Krishnamurti (see Figure 9).

Krishnamurti's teaching is an inquiry into the whole phenomenon of existence, including bondage to identification and how that bondage precludes freedom to participate in a sacred, timeless, and limitless consciousness, which he also refers to as love. He begins with a diagnosis of how individuals are controlled and limited by thought, with a demonstration of how all inventions of thought, whether through religion, science, or self-reflection, chain individuals to the past, to time, and to the known. Then he asks if one can learn for oneself whether there is something unnamable, beyond time and not created by thought, which is not an illusion. His deliberations then move from knowledge to inquiry, from thought to observation. He warns that inquiry into the unperceivable and the unknowable must always be new, residing in the present

Figure 9 J. Krishnamurti, 1977. Photo by Frances McCann, courtesy Krishnamurti Foundations.

moment, without identification with patterns of thought that are inexorable bondage to the past. Properly, such inquiry cannot depend upon authority, experiences, or knowledge, which are the very essence of thought. Instead, inquiry must examine the possibility of finding a mind that is utterly quiet, without control, discipline, or effort. Can the mind, the whole organic structure, be completely still and utterly quiet, as well as empty of all contents, of all that it knows? Krishnamurti responds to his own question: only if the mind can observe its own limitation and in that seeing, bring about the dissolution of the limitation. Through direct observation of self without an image of oneself as observer, one enters a timeless, spaceless silence that is both sacred and free, serving as the ground of compassion and love.

Krishnamurti's insights into how the mind operates reveal the problems caused when individuals assume that they have actual relationships with other humans. Life in a world of images derived from thought, ideas, theories, and symbols separates individuals from real engagement with others. In effect, each person's images of others are in relationship to others' images of that person, while the humans attached to each image are not in relationship (Krishnamurti 1969: 58). This separation, division, and contradiction inevitably bring conflict, both within a person and among people, because thinking and acting with images and symbols constitutes "psychological thought" and the "psychological structure of society," both of which prohibit genuine awareness and genuine relationship with others (Krishnamurti 1969: 59–60). In short, to Krishnamurti, "Freedom from images is real freedom" (Krishnamurti 1982a: 41).

In his explanation of the development of consciousness and its attendant growth of being, Krishnamurti advises an investigation into the limitations of any system, whether specific techniques, religious authorities, or contemplative traditions. He asserts that truth is a pathless land and that true meditation involves freedom from the known, realities that can be apprehended only when one finds the light of self-inquiry in oneself. Only an instantaneous psychological revolution can bring understanding of these truths and bring real transformation in individuals, relationships, and society.

Krishnamurti and his teaching remain in conversation with thinkers in many fields and his insights have proven important for consideration of transformation of consciousness. Consistent with many Asian teachings, he maintains that the aim and responsibility of human life is to rid the self of the illusions of conditioning, through careful examination of how the mind operates. When the mind becomes completely attentive, not bound by the images of thought, then real awareness and real freedom appear. Relationships within the self and with others no longer depend upon images of self, images of others, and memory. One moves beyond self-hypnosis and illusion to live in the present, with a clarity that allows the perception of truth and "bridges the gap between the mind and the heart" (Krishnamurti 1970: 22–3).

Krishnamurti's focus on inquiry opens a critical lens on self-observation, valorizes holistic learning, and invalidates dependence upon conceptual universes and linguistic thought. With these themes, his teaching presages current ontologies and epistemologies in several fields, including psychology, consciousness studies, and philosophical paradigms, a review of which is beyond the scope of this Element. Parallel to several postmodern paradigmatic shifts in human sciences, religious studies, and philosophy, he claims that sincere personal inquiry is the only valid process for self-understanding. When we consider current directions of thought and practice (Vaysse 1978; Ravindra 1999; Conge 2004; de Llosa 2006; Brierty 2007; Ramana 2014; Bourgeault 2021; and Metzner 2022), we find that Krishnamurti is prescient in his description of self-inquiry into truth as both epistemological goal and *summum bonum*.

In the midst of confrontation with the chaotic nature of the present world and its endless dilemmas, Krishnamurti presents a message that situates interdependence as underlying reality, focuses on relationship as the basis of human existence, and calls for re-sacralization of all life. In this integral approach to understanding the human condition, he joins with other change agents (Berry 1999; Merchant 2005; Dalai Lama 2011; Macy & Johnstone 2012; Goodall & Abrams 2021; and Nhat Hanh 2020) who seek human and more-than-human flourishing. Krishnamurti offers a paradigm for transformation, which includes an epistemology that rests on individual freedom, deconditioning, and learning through perception, not belief; an ontology that posits a nondual whole underlying all consciousness and manifestation; a methodology that requires investigation through sincere inquiry; and an axiology that values joint liberation of self and the collective.

Krishnamurti rejected the role of guru and forbade the establishment of any organization whose members would join in his name. The Krishnamurti Foundations around the globe promote his teachings, but do not promote the man himself. At the same time, he has served as a beacon for many who search for authentic insight into the human condition through rigorous self-inquiry. In this way he was a World Teacher, but not a guru.

As Krishnamurti spoke simply and directly to those who listened, he functioned and still functions as a persuasive influence in the exploration of universal themes surrounding the human condition, including thought, conditioning, identification, relationships, fear, creativity, affection, and love. In his diagnosis of the ills of contemporary life, he was stark and unrelenting. Yet, in his vision of a new consciousness, he proffered hope for transformation and transmutation for all individuals and for the world.

> Your consciousness is not yours. It is the consciousness of all humanity, because what you think, your beliefs, your sensations, your reactions, your pain, your sorrow, your insecurity, your gods, and so on, are shared by all humanity. (Krishnamurti 1983a: 37)

References

Balasundaram, S. 2012. *Non-Guru Guru: My Years with J. Krishnamurti*. Ojai, CA: Edwin House.

Benjamin, H. 1971. *Basic Self-Knowledge: Based on the Gurdjieff System of Development with Reference to the Writings of Krishnamurti*. York Beach, ME: Samuel Weiser.

Berry, T. 1999. *The Great Work: One Way into the Future*. New York: Three Rivers Press.

Besant, A. 1889. "Why I Became a Theosophist." Two lectures given in the Hall of Science, London, August 4 and 11, 1889. Adyar: Archives of the Theosophical Society.

Besant, A. & C. W. Leadbeater. 1924. *The Lives of Alcyone*. 2 Vols. Adyar: Theosophical Publishing.

Blavatsky, H. P. 1877. *Isis Unveiled*. New York: J. W. Bouton.

Blavatsky, H. P. 1888. *The Secret Doctrine: The Synthesis of Science, Religion, and Philosophy*. London: Theosophical Publishing.

Bohm, D. 1985. *Unfolding Meaning: A Weekend of Dialogue*. London: Routledge.

Bohm, D. 1994. *Thought as a System*. London: Routledge.

Bohm, D. 1996. *On Dialogue*. London: Routledge.

Bohm, D. 2002. *Wholeness and the Implicate Order*. London: Routledge.

Bohm, D. & F. D. Peat. 1987. *Science, Order, and Creativity: A Dramatic New Look at the Creative Roots of Science and Life*. New York: Bantam.

Bourgeault, C. 2016. *The Heart of Centering Prayer: Nondual Christianity in Theory and Practice*. Boulder, CO: Shambhala.

Bourgeault, C. 2020. *Eye of the Heart: A Spiritual Journey into the Imaginal Realm*. Boulder, CO: Shambhala.

Bourgeault, C. 2021. *Mystical Courage: Commentaries on Selected Contemplative Exercises by G. I. Gurdjieff, as Compiled by Joseph Azize*. Rhinebeck, NY: Red Elixir.

Brierty, L. 2007. *The Self-Inquiry Process: Using Powerful Questions to Awaken Awareness*. New York: Cosimo.

Bruntrup, G. & L. Jaskolla (eds.). 2017. *Panpsychism: Contemporary Perspectives*. New York: Oxford University Press.

Burnier, R. 1995. "J. Krishnamurti." *The Indian Theosophist* 93, nos. 5–6 (May–June): 104–7.

Campbell, B. F. 1980. *Ancient Wisdom Revived: A History of the Theosophical Movement*. Berkeley, CA: University of California.

Chalmers, D. J. 2010. *The Character of Consciousness*. New York: Oxford University Press.

Conge, M. 2004. *Inner Octaves*. Toronto: Dolmen Meadow Editions.

Costandi, M. 2016. *Neuroplasticity*. Cambridge, MA: MIT Press.

Dalai Lama. 2011. *Beyond Religion: Ethics for a Whole World*. New York: Houghton Mifflin.

Damasio, A. 2022. *Feeling & Knowing: Making Minds Conscious*. New York: Vintage.

De Llosa, P. 2006. *The Practice of Presence*. Sandpoint, ID: Morning Light Press.

Eisler, R. & D. P. Fry. 2019. *Nurturing our Humanity: How Domination and Partnership Shape our Brains, Lives, and Future*. New York: Oxford University Press.

Faivre, A. & J. Needleman (eds.). 1995. *Modern Esoteric Spirituality*. New York: Crossroad.

Ferrer, J. 2002. *Revisioning Transpersonal Theory: A Participatory Vision of Human Spirituality*. Albany, NY: State University of New York Press.

Ferrer, J. 2017. *Participation and the Mystery: Transpersonal Essays in Psychology, Education, and Religion*. Albany, NY: State University of New York.

Forbes, S. 1995. "Education as a Religious Activity." *The Theosophist* 116, no. 8 (May): 338–47.

Godwin, J. 1994. *The Theosophical Enlightenment*. Albany, NY: State University of New York.

Goodall, J. & D. Abrams. 2021. *The Book of Hope: A Survival Guide for Trying Times*. New York: Celadon.

Grof, S. 1993. *The Holotropic Mind: The Three Levels of Human Consciousness and How They Shape Our Lives*. San Francisco, CA: Harper.

Grof, S. 1998. *The Cosmic Game: Explorations of the Frontiers of Human Consciousness*. Albany, NY: State University of New York Press.

Hanegraaff, W. J. (ed.). 2006. *Dictionary of Gnosis and Western Esotericism*. Boston, MA: Brill Academic.

Hindupedia. 2024. "Rajju Sarpa Nyaya." www.hindupedia.com/en/Nyayas. Accessed September 11, 2024.

Holroyd, S. 1991. *Krishnamurti: The Man, the Mystery, and the Message*. Shaftesbury, UK: Element.

Jayakar, P. 1986. *Krishnamurti: A Biography*. New York: Penguin.

Jayakar, P. 1995. *Fire in the Mind: Dialogues with J. Krishnamurti*. New Delhi: Penguin.

Jayakar, P. & S. Patwardan (eds.). 1981. *Within the Mind: On J. Krishnamurti.* New Delhi: Krishnamurti Foundation India.

Jones, C. A. 2010. "Krishnamurti Foundations." In J. G. Melton & M. Bauman (eds.), *Religions of the World: A Comprehensive Encyclopedia of Beliefs and Practices*, 2nd ed., vol. 4, 1661–3. Santa Barbara, CA: ABC-Clio.

Jones, C. A. & J. D. Ryan. 2007. *Encyclopedia of Hinduism.* New York: Facts on File.

Krishna, P. 1995. "The Religious Mind to J. Krishnamurti." Seminar. December 14. Adyar: The Theosophical Society. Not recorded.

Krishna, P. 2015. *A Jewel on a Silver Platter.* Ojai, CA: Peepal Leaves.

Krishna, P. 2023. "Reflections on Krishnamurti's First and Last Freedom." Seminar. June 24. Hosted by Krishnamurti Foundation India, Varanasi.

Krishnamurthy, K. (ed.). 1995. *Krishnamurti for Beginners: An Anthology.* Madras: Krishnamurti Foundation India.

Krishnamurti, J. 1953. *Education and the Significance of Life.* San Francisco, CA: Harper & Row.

Krishnamurti, J. 1954. *The First and Last Freedom.* San Francisco, CA: HarperSanFrancisco.

Krishnamurti, J. 1960. *Commentaries on Living, from the Notebooks of J. Krishnamurti*, 3 vols., D. Rajagopal, ed. Wheaton, IL: Theosophical Publishing.

Krishnamurti, J. 1969. *Freedom from the Known.* New York: Harper and Row.

Krishnamurti, J. 1970. *The Only Revolution.* New York: Harper and Row.

Krishnamurti, J. 1971. *The Flight of the Eagle.* New York: Harper and Row.

Krishnamurti, J. 1972. *You Are the World.* Madras: Krishnamurti Foundation India.

Krishnamurti, J. 1973. *The Awakening of Intelligence.* San Francisco, CA: Harper.

Krishnamurti, J. (pseud. Alcyone). 1974a. *At the Feet of the Master.* Wheaton, IL: Theosophical Publishing.

Krishnamurti, J. 1974b. *Krishnamurti on Education.* New York: Harper & Row.

Krishnamurti, J. 1979. *The Wholeness of Life.* San Francisco, CA: Harper and Row.

Krishnamurti, J. 1981. *Rajghat Questions and Answers.* Video. Krishnamurti Foundation America. Ojai, CA: Krishnamurti Foundation of America.

Krishnamurti, J. 1982a. *The Network of Thought.* San Francisco, CA: Harper & Row.

Krishnamurti, J. 1982b. *Ojai Questions and Answers.* Video. Krishnamurti Foundation America. Ojai, CA: Krishnamurti Foundation of America.

Krishnamurti, J. 1983a. *Mind without Measure*. London: Krishnamurti Foundation Trust.

Krishnamurti, J. 1983b. *Saanen, Questions and Answers*. Video. Krishnamurti Foundation America. Ojai, CA: Krishnamurti Foundation of America.

Krishnamurti, J. 1984. *Saanen, Questions and Answers*. Video. Krishnamurti Foundation America. Ojai, CA: Krishnamurti Foundation of America.

Krishnamurti, J. 1985. *Rajghat, Questions and Answers*. Video. Krishnamurti Foundation America. Ojai, CA: Krishnamurti Foundation of America

Krishnamurti, J. 1991. *A Wholly Different Way of Living: In Dialogue with Professor Allan W. Anderson*. London: Victor Gollancz.

Krishnamurti, J. 1996a. *Total Freedom: The Essential Krishnamurti*. San Francisco, CA: Harper.

Krishnamurti, J. 1996b. *Questioning Krishnamurti*. London: HarperCollins.

Krishnamurti, J. 1999. *This Light in Oneself: True Meditation*. Boston, MA: Shambhala.

Krishnamurti, J. 2002 [1979]. *Meditations*. Boston, MA: Shambhala.

Krishnamurti, J. 2014. *The World Within: You Are the Story of Humanity*. Ojai, CA: Krishnamurti Foundation of America.

Krishnamurti, J. 2015.*Unconditioning and Education: The Need for a Radical Approach*, vol. I. Ojai, CA: Krishnamurti Foundation of America.

Krishnamurti, J. & D. Bohm. 1986. *The Future of Humanity: A Conversation*. New York: Harper and Row.

Krishnamurti, J. & D. Bohm. 1999. *The Limits of Thought: Discussions between J. Krishnamurti and David Bohm*. New York: Routledge.

Krishnamurti, J. & D. Bohm. 2014. *The Ending of Time*, rev. ed., 1985. San Francisco, CA: Harper.

Landau, I. 2019. "Krishnamurti's Insistence on Pathless Enlightenment: A Critique." *Journal of Indian Philosophy and Religion* 24: 31–55.

Laszlo, E. 2017. *The Intelligence of the Cosmos: Why Are We Here?* Rochester, VT: Inner Traditions.

Lee, Kristy. 2024. Personal Communication with Archive & Publications Director, Ojai, CA: Krishnamurti Foundation of America. September 6, 2024.

Lee, R. E. M. 2016. *Knocking at the Open Door: My Years with J. Krishnamurti*, 2nd ed. Bloomington, IN: Balboa.

Lee, R. E. M. 2020. *J. Krishnamurti's Process: Probing the Mystery*. Ojai, CA: Edwin House.

Lutyens, M. 1975. *Krishnamurti: The Years of Awakening*. London: John Murray Publishers.

Lutyens, M. 1983. *Krishnamurti: The Years of Fulfilment*. New York: Farrar Straus Giroux.

Lutyens, M. 1988. *Krishnamurti: The Open Door.* New York: Farrar Straus Giroux.

Lutyens, M. 1990. *The Life and Death of Krishnamurti.* London: John Murray Publishers.

Lutyens, M. 1996. *Krishnamurti and the Rajagopals.* Ojai, CA: Krishnamurti Foundation of America.

Macy, J. & C. Johnstone. 2012. *Active Hope: How to Face the Mess We're in without Going Crazy.* Novato, CA: New World Library.

Malin, S. 2001. *Nature Loves to Hide: Quantum Physics and Reality, A Western Perspective.* New York: Oxford University Press.

Malin, S. 2004. *The Eye that Sees Itself.* Sandpoint, ID: Morning Light Press.

Mathews, F. 2023. *The Dao of Civilization: A Letter to China.* New York: Anthem Press.

Mehta, R. 1979. *J. Krishnamurti and the Nameless Experience*, 3rd ed. Delhi: Motilal Banarsidass.

Mehta, R. 1987. *The Secret of Self-Transformation: A Synthesis of Tantra and Yoga.* Delhi: Motilal Banarsidass.

Melton, J. G. (ed.). 2017. *Melton's Encyclopedia of American Religions*, 9th ed. Framingham Hills, MI: Gale.

Mendizza, M., director. 1985. *Challenge of Change.* Film. 80 minutes. Ojai, CA: Krishnamurti Foundation of America.

Mendizza, M., director. 1990. *With a Silent Mind.* Film. 120 minutes. Ojai, CA: Krishnamurti Foundation of America.

Merchant, C. 2005. *Radical Ecology: The Search for a Livable World*, 2nd ed. New York: Taylor & Francis.

Metzner, R. 2022. *The Unfolding Self: Varieties of Transformative Experience.* Santa Fe, NM: Synergetic Press.

Moody, D. E. 2011. *The Unconditioned Mind: J. Krishnamurti and the Oak Grove School.* Wheaton, IL: Quest.

Moody, D. E. 2016. *An Uncommon Collaboration: David Bohm and J. Krishnamurti.* Ojai, CA: Alpha Centauri.

Murphet, H. 1975. *When Daylight Comes: A Biography of Helena Petrovna Blavatsky.* Wheaton, Il: TheosophicalPublishing.

Needleman, J. 1970. *The New Religions.* New York: Dutton.

Nethercot, A. H. 1963. *The Last Four Lives of Annie Besant.* Chicago, IL: University of Chicago Press.

Nhat Hanh, Thich. 2020. *Interbeing: The 14 Mindfulness Trainings of Engaged Buddhism.* Berkeley, CA: Parallax.

Patrik, L. E. 1995. "Perilous Sitting." Paper presented at the Birth Centenary of Krishnamurti, Miami University, Oxford, Ohio, May 19.

Penrose, R., S. Hameroff, & S. Kak (eds.). 2017. *Consciousness and the Universe: Quantum Physics, Evolution, Brain, & Mind*. Cambridge, MA: Cosmology Science.

De Purucker, G. 1979. *Fundamentals of the Esoteric Philosophy*. Pasadena, CA: Theosophical University Press.

Rahula, W. 1996. "Are You Not Saying What the Buddha Said?" In J. Krishnamurti (ed.), *Questioning Krishnamurti: J. Krishnamurti in Dialogue*, 18–38. London: Thorsons.

Ramana, Maharshi. 2014. *How to Practice Self Inquiry*. Freedom Religion Press.

Ravindra, R. 1995. *Krishnamurti: Two Birds on One Tree*. Wheaton, IL: Theosophical Publishing.

Ravindra, R. 1999. *Heart without Measure: Work with Madame de Salzmann*. Halifax, Canada: Shaila Press.

Ricard, M. & W. Singer. 2017. *Beyond the Self: Conversations between Buddhism and Neuroscience*. Cambridge, MA: The MIT Press.

Sabzevary, A. 2008. "Choiceless Awareness through Psychological Freedom in the Philosophy of Krishnamurti." PhD dissertation, California Institute of Integral Studies.

Samdhong Rinpoche with M. Mendizza. 2017. *Always Awakening: Buddha's Realization, Krishnamurti's Insight*. Solvang, CA: Michael Mendizza.

Sanat, A. 1999. *The Inner Life of Krishnamurti*. Wheaton, IL: Theosophical Publishing.

Santucci, J. A. 2006. "Theosophical Society." In W. Hanegraaff (ed.), *Dictionary of Gnosis and Western Esotericism*, 1114–23. Boston, MA: Brill Academic.

Sloss, R. R. 1991. *Lives in the Shadow with J. Krishnamurti*. Reading, MA: Addison-Wesley.

Smith, H. 1996. "Can One Have Lucidity in this Confused World?" In J. Krishnamurti (ed.), *Questioning Krishnamurti: J. Krishnamurti in Dialogue*, 200–14. London: Thorsons.

Suzuki, S. 1970. *Zen Mind, Beginner's Mind*. New York: Weatherhill.

Tillett, G. 1982. *The Elder Brother: A Biography of Charles Webster Leadbeater*. London: Routledge & Kegan Paul.

Trungpa, C. 1987. *Cutting Through Spiritual Materialism*. Boston, MA: Shambhala.

Tubali, S. 2023. *The Transformative Philosophical Dialogue: From Classical Dialogues to Jiddu Krishnamurti's Method*. Cham, Switzerland: Springer Nature.

Van der Kolk, B. A. 2014. *The Body Keeps the Score: Brain, Mind, and Body in the Healing of Trauma*. New York: Penguin.

Van der Struijf, J. & C. Van der Struijf. 2000. *The Concise Guide to Krishnamurti: A Study Companion and Index to the Recorded Teachings (1979–1986)*. Ojai, CA: Krishnamurti Foundation of America.

Varela, F. J., E. Thompson, & E. Rosch. 2016. *The Embodied Mind: Cognitive Science and Human Experience*, rev. edn. Cambridge, MA: MIT Press.

Vaysse, J. 1978. *Toward Awakening: An Approach to the Teaching Left by Gurdjieff*. San Francisco, CA: Far West.

Vernon, R. 2000. *Star in the East: Krishnamurti, The Invention of a Messiah*. Boulder, CO: Sentient Publications.

Washington, P. 1995. *Madame Blavatsky's Baboon: A History of the Mystics, Mediums, and Misfits Who Brought Spiritualism to America*. New York: Schocken.

Weber, R. 1996. "Why is Your Teaching So Difficult to Live?" In J. Krishnamurti (ed.), *Questioning Krishnamurti: J. Krishnamurti in Dialogue*, 215–35. London: Thorsons.

Wessinger, C. L. 1988. *Annie Besant and Progressive Messianism 1847–1933*. New York: Edwin Mellen.

Wilber, K. 2001. *No Boundary: Eastern and Western Approaches to Personal Growth*. Boston, MA: Shambhala.

Supplemental Resources

Aurobindo, Sri. 1972. *The Synthesis of Yoga*. Pondicherry: All India Press.

Boag, A. 2019. "The 'Lost Word' Key and Esoteric Eschatology: Blavatsky's Gnosis the Core of Krishnamurti's Teaching." In G. Trompf (ed.), *The Gnostic World*, 48–98. New York: Routledge.

Buber, M. 1970. *I and Thou*, trans. W. Kaufman. New York: Simon & Schuster.

Combs, A. 2009. *Consciousness Explained Better: Towards an Integral Understanding of the Multifaceted Nature of Consciousness*. St. Paul, MN: Paragon House.

De Quincey, C. 2005. *Radical Knowing: Understanding Consciousness through Relationship*. Rochester, VT: Park Street Press.

Ferrer, J. N. & J. H. Sherman (eds.). 2008. *The Participatory Turn: Spirituality, Mysticism, Religious Studies*. Albany, NY: State University of New York Press.

Feuerstein, G. 1987. *Structures of Consciousness: The Genius of Jean Gebser*. Lower Lake, CA: Integral.

Gergen, K. 2009. *An Invitation to Social Construction*, 2nd ed. Thousand Oaks, CA: Sage.

Heron, J. 1996. *Co-operative Inquiry: Research into the Human Condition*. Thousand Oaks, CA: Sage.

Heron, J. & P. Reason. 1997. "A Participatory Inquiry Paradigm." *Qualitative Inquiry* 3: 274–94.

Holroyd, S. 1980. *The Quest of the Quiet Mind: The Philosophy of Krishnamurti*. Wellingborough, UK: Aquarian Press.

Huxley, A. 1944. *The Perennial Philosophy*. New York: Harper and Row.

Huxley, A. 1954. "Foreword." In J. Krishnamurti (ed.), *The First and Last Freedom*, 9–18. San Francisco, CA: HarperSanFrancisco.

James, W. 1929 [1902]. *The Varieties of Religious Experience*. New York: Modern Library.

James, W. 1996 [1911]. *Some Problems of Philosophy: A Beginning of an Introduction to Philosophy*. Lincoln, NE: University of Nebraska Press.

Jones, C. 1997. "J. Krishnamurti on the Religious Life." In D. Singh (ed.), *Spiritual Traditions: Essential Ways for Living*, n.p. Bangalore: United Theological College.

Jones, C. 2015. "Techniqueless Meditation: J. Krishnamurti's This Light in Oneself." In L. Komjathy (ed.), *Contemplative Literature: A Comparative Sourcebook on Meditation and Contemplative Prayer*, 645–702. Albany, NY: SUNY Press.

Krishnamurti, J. 1947. *Authentic Report of Sixteen Talks Given in 1945 & 1946 by Krishnamurti*. Ojai, CA: Krishnamurti Writings.

Krishnamurti, J. 1970. *The Second Penguin Krishnamurti Reader*, (ed.) M. Lutyens. New York: Penguin.

Krishnamurti, J. 1974. *This Matter of Culture*. London: Victor Gollancz

Krishnamurti, J. 1975. *Talks in Saanen 1974*. Wembley, UK: Krishnamurti Foundation Trust.

Krishnamurti, J. 1988. *Commentaries on Living. Third Series*. Wheaton, IL: Theosophical Publishing.

Krishnamurti, J. 1991. *On Freedom*. San Francisco, CA: Harper.

Krishnamurti, J. 1993. *On Mind and Thought*. San Francisco, CA: Harper.

Lincoln, Y., S. Lynham, & E. Guba. 2011. "Paradigmatic Controversies, Contradictions, and Emerging Confluences, Revisited." In N. Denzin & Y. Lincoln (eds.), *The Sage Handbook of Qualitative Research*, 4th ed., 97–128. Thousand Oaks, CA: Sage.

Mendizza, M. (ed.). 2020. *Unconditionally Free*. Ojai, CA: Krishnamurti Foundation of America.

Meyer, M. 2003. "Gnosticism, Gnostics, and the Gnostic Bible." In W. Barnstone & M. Meyer (eds.), *The Gnostic Bible*, 1–19. Boston, MA: Shambhala.

Miller, H. 1969. *The Books in My Life*. New York: New Directions.

Narayan, S. 1995. "Religion Lies in Living." *The Indian Theosophist* 93, nos. 5–6: 108–10.

References

Ransom, J. 1938. *A Short History of the Theosophical Society*. Adyar: The Theosophical Publishing.

Rogers, C. 1980. *A Way of Being*. Boston, MA: Houghton Mifflin.

Schuon, F. 1984. *The Transcendent Unity of Religions*. Wheaton, IL: Theosophical Publishing.

Spretnak, C. 2011. *Relational Reality: New Discoveries of Interrelatedness that Are Transforming the Modern World*. Topsham, ME: Green Horizon.

Wilber, K. 2000. *Integral Psychology*. Boston, MA: Shambhala.

Wilber, K. 2006. *Integral Spirituality*. Boston, MA: Shambhala.

Young, A. 1976. *The Reflexive Universe: Evolution of Consciousness*. New York: Delacorte Press.

Zaehner, R. C. 1960. *Hindu and Muslim Mysticism*. New York: Schocken.

Acknowledgments

I am grateful to the California Institute of Integral Studies for supporting this research through a sabbatical leave and professional development funds. For the hundreds of graduate students who have joined me in collaborative self-inquiry over many years, I remain edified and thankful. For sharing his unique understanding and embodiment of Krishnamurti's message, pranams to Padmanabhan Krishna. For tutelage in interpreting Krishnamurti's teaching and her editorial advice, I am deeply indebted to Margaret Dodd. For Rebecca Moore's impeccable editorial eye and infinite patience, I am deeply appreciative. My gratitude extends to Cory Fisher and Kristy Lee, who have served as Director of Publications and Archive of the Krishnamurti Foundation of America, Ojai, California, for their help in several areas of research. And for the nourishing conversations with faculty and staff of the Krishnamurti Study Centre and Vasanta College, Rajghat, throughout my time in Varanasi as a Fulbright scholar, I retain warm memories and much affection.

Cambridge Elements =

New Religious Movements

Founding Editor
†James R. Lewis
Wuhan University

The late James R. Lewis was a Professor of Philosophy at Wuhan University, China. He was the author or co-author of 128 articles and reference book entries, and editor or co-editor of 50 books. He was also the general editor for the *Alternative Spirituality and Religion Review* and served as the associate editor for the *Journal of Religion and Violence*. His prolific publications include *The Cambridge Companion to Religion and Terrorism* (Cambridge University Press 2017) and *Falun Gong: Spiritual Warfare and Martyrdom* (Cambridge University Press 2018).

Series Editor
Rebecca Moore
San Diego State University

Rebecca Moore is Emerita Professor of Religious Studies at San Diego State University. She has written and edited numerous books and articles on Peoples Temple and the Jonestown tragedy. Publications include *Beyond Brainwashing: Perspectives on Cultic Violence* (Cambridge University Press 2018) and *Peoples Temple and Jonestown in the Twenty-First Century* (Cambridge University Press 2022). She is reviews editor for *Nova Religio*, the quarterly journal on new and emergent religions published by the University of Pennsylvania Press.

About the Series

Elements in New Religious Movements go beyond cult stereotypes and popular prejudices to present new religions and their adherents in a scholarly and engaging manner. Case studies of individual groups, such as Transcendental Meditation and Scientology, provide in-depth consideration of some of the most well known, and controversial, groups. Thematic examinations of women, children, science, technology, and other topics focus on specific issues unique to these groups. Historical analyses locate new religions in specific religious, social, political, and cultural contexts. These examinations demonstrate why some groups exist in tension with the wider society and why others live peaceably in the mainstream. The series highlights the differences, as well as the similarities, within this great variety of religious expressions. To discuss contributing to this series please contact Professor Moore.

Cambridge Elements

New Religious Movements

Elements in the Series

The New Witches of the West: Tradition, Liberation, and Power
Ethan Doyle White

The New Age Movement
Margrethe Løøv

Black Hebrew Israelites
Michael T. Miller

Anticultism in France: Scientology, Religious Freedom, and the Future of New and Minority Religions
Donald A. Westbrook

The Production of Entheogenic Communities in the United States
Brad Stoddard

Managing Religion and Religious Changes in Iran: A Socio-Legal Analysis
Sajjad Adeliyan Tous and James T. Richardson

Children in New Religious Movements
Sanja Nilsson

The Sacred Force of Star Wars Jedi
William Sims Bainbridge

Mormonism
Matthew Bowman

Jehovah's Witnesses
Jolene Chu and Ollimatti Peltonen

Wearing Their Faith: New Religious Movements, Dress, and Fashion in America
Lynn S. Neal

J. Krishnamurti: Self-Inquiry, Awakening, and Transformation
Constance A. Jones

A full series listing is available at: www.cambridge.org/ENRM

For EU product safety concerns, contact us at Calle de José Abascal, 56–1°, 28003 Madrid, Spain or eugpsr@cambridge.org.

www.ingramcontent.com/pod-product-compliance
Lightning Source LLC
LaVergne TN
LVHW020350260326
834688LV00045B/1648